Christian Mothers
Reveal Their
JOYS
and
SORROWS

Interviews and Photographs by Roger Elwood

STANDARD PUBLISHING
Cincinnati, Ohio   2970

Library of Congress Catalog Card Number: 79-64765

ISBN: 0-87239-372-0
© 1979. The STANDARD PUBLISHING COMPANY, Cincinnati, Ohio
Division of STANDEX INTERNATIONAL CORPORATION.
Printed in U.S.A.

DEDICATION

To Carol Ferntheil, who shared with us her life in the Savior through several years of joyous ministry together.

While completing production of this Christian mothers book, Carol lost her life in the tragic plane crash of May 25, 1979, near O'Hare airport. She was enroute to participate in the American Booksellers Convention in Los Angeles.

Carol was an exceptional personality. Her ministry among us as Director of Product Development will remain unforgettable.

The gentle philosophy of Mrs. Ferntheil underlies this book. It was her last earthly production. We commend it to you.

The Publishers

A word of special thanks to the thirty-four mothers who have so graciously scheduled their time for interviews with Roger Elwood. They have spoken with openness and freedom. Standard Publishing is pleased to print their frank opinions with the understanding that these do not necessarily reflect the policies or philosophy of the Company.

The Editors

Contents

Introduction

Being a mother is all encompassing. A woman must also be a good wife, friend, and much else in order to be a source of strength and stability within the family circle.

None of us—male or female—know what the future holds when we extend the boundaries of our self-oriented world to include a husband or a wife, and then children. There can be great joy, the most sublime ecstasy known to human beings this side of Heaven, or there can be unrelieved pain and suffering, but, for most, there is some joy, some pain, some suffering, in unequal doses.

This book attempts to present a broad tapestry of situations, opinions, and so on. The unifying thread is that no one can say being a wife, a mother, is without its tragedies or its triumphs. In some instances we have concentrated solely on the *mother* part of a woman's family life. In others we have leaned more toward the *wife* part. The overall effect, we hope, is a broader portrait of motherhood, in all its different hues, than has generally been available specifically for Christian readers.

We think you will find much with which to identify: whether with the problems of raising retarded children; or the sorrow of losing a son in a tragic plane crash; or being married to a man who has been horribly disfigured; or, simply, the more commonplace aspects of raising children and being a wife.

The women in this book have opened some very private doors to their inner selves and they ask you, now, to step through as an invited guest.

Roger Elwood
Westlake Village, CA

Dorothy Engstrom

I was an only child, and a very unhealthy, sickly child. My mother took me from one specialist to another throughout my childhood. Then I went away to college where I fell in love with a very brilliant, fantastic young man named Ted Engstrom. We had a three-year courtship while attending Taylor University. During that time Ted underwent a remarkable conversion. Afterwards we really considered seriously our future together. We were convinced the Lord wanted us to marry.

Were you, yourself, born again at the time?

Yes indeed. I came from a strong Christian family, and I had accepted Christ at an early age.

What had Ted's background been?

He was raised in the Christian and Missionary Alliance Church at Cleveland, Ohio.

But not born again?

No, and he was very anti in those days. His parents sent him away to school to be reformed. The first year he was there, however, he was asked to leave.

He was? Why?

Just general rebellion all the time. Then he "found the Lord" at one of the special meetings we had in chapel. It completely changed his life, this remarkable encounter. He had to ask for permission from the university to come back to school. He confided that his aim in life was someday to be on the board of Taylor University.

And, sure enough, later he was not only that but also Chairman of the Board for many years, and one of two life members!

The irony is interesting.

Yes, very interesting. One Saturday afternoon I asked the Dean of Women if I could leave the university grounds very briefly and walk downtown with Ted. She replied, "Oh, no, Miss Weaver, you know this isn't going to last." And it lasted forty years.

Terribly optimistic, wasn't it?

Very. But then we were married and moved off the university grounds. We continued to work there for awhile, then moved to Grand Rapids. All this time, considering all I'd been through as a child, I just knew that it'd be very difficult for me to get pregnant. I was continually anxious about that.

Ted was editor of Zondervan Publishing House then, and Pat and Mary Zondervan were very dear friends of ours. They, too, couldn't have children, and they were in the process of adopting. Ted and I began to think in that direction.

You can imagine how I must have felt, doing The Children's Bible Hour as Aunt Betty, telling Bible stories for seven years. Every Saturday morning I was with all these little children, just adoring every minute, and yet knowing that perhaps I would never have any children of my own.

By the time we were married six years, Ted was in the service, stationed with the Army camps out in California. I was so bitter and unhappy that, when my best friend had a baby, I couldn't even go to the hospital to see her. While I would have been glad for her, I would have once again found myself in the midst of

10

regret that I couldn't have a baby as she did. I just wanted a baby more than anything else in the world.

Did you feel, at any point, that you were letting Ted down?

Oh, sure. While he wasn't anybody special, then, he was pretty special to me, and I yearned so much to give him a child.

Then he was in an accident, and I spent a long time by his side in the barracks. He was in a jeep and the jeep skidded on a slippery road out in the desert. The jeep flipped over four times, and he thought he was a goner. He had contusions on the head and neck, and a very bad hip injury which plagued him for years. He had surgery, and now everything's fine.

Anyhow, we were in Palm Springs, and the girl at the desk next to me went to Los Angeles and had an abortion one weekend. Her boyfriend gave her the money to pay for it. And several of the other girls would go into bars and take their children with them, and leave the youngsters to go to sleep on the bar benches.

I was so bitter, not having any children, and there they were with children, and treating them so poorly.

As if all this wasn't bad enough, I ended up in emergency surgery in the Army hospital. I was hemorrhaging badly. A tumor was causing this. I had a very rare condition as a child that I won't go into. But I ended up having surgery. After the surgery, there was no hope at all that I'd ever be a natural mother. We talked to different doctors about adoption, knowing that we were not the kind of people to go through life without a family.

Ironically, I was the one to discharge Ted from the Army. I was head of the discharge section. We had pictures in papers all over the country. I was the first wife who had ever discharged her husband with such great joy, believe me.

We returned home to Grand Rapids and Ted resumed his editorship at Zondervan. Pat and Mary had just gotten their son, Bob, so Mary introduced us to the head of the home. We went through the nursery looking at all the babies. Ted would look at one after another, asking, "How about this one? Is this a boy or a girl? We really don't care, but is this one adoptable?" And so forth, baby after baby.

Then we went home. Two weeks later, just two weeks later, they called us. They said they had never had a couple that were yearning so for a baby—that we could come the next morning and pick up our baby!

11

Well, she didn't know us very well, because there wouldn't have been any sleep that night if we had had to wait. We said, "We'll be right over." We were in the process of entertaining three couples from church, including our pastor and his wife, and so I was having a dinner party that night. We didn't do the dishes or anything. We dropped everything and went over to get our baby. Later we had a great time because all the other couples wanted to be in on the excitement, too.

I had never had any experience with tiny babies, but our pastor's wife had had five. She had to tell me how to make the hole in the nipple bigger so he could get some nourishment, and it was a very interesting, exciting evening. I ended up sitting awake, all night, holding him. I never, never put him down that first night.

It was a quick decision on the part of those at the home. They hadn't really investigated us or interviewed us in any great depth. Realizing this, I suppose, two investigators came by at 8:30 the next morning, after I'd been up all night. They wanted to see if we were going to work out as parents. They walked in and chatted for awhile, then I went out to the kitchen to fix coffee, and they followed me. Everything was, of course, in a shambles after the previous evening's dinner. I hadn't straightened *anything* yet. Some apple pie was left over. It was the first apple pie I had ever made, and the *last* one that I've ever made. I shared it with them along with their coffee. On the adoption recommendation we later read, "Anybody who can make apple pie like that will be a good mother."

I never bothered to make another one all the rest of our forty years of married life because I wanted that to be a special story we'd always remember in that way.

I adored our baby, Gordon Paul. He was five weeks old. Every place we took him, my eyes were always on him. One time we were having dinner in a restaurant, and I just couldn't take my eyes off that baby. Ted said, "I knew you would be that way." Though he didn't say this in any derogatory way at all, it kind of hit me and I thought, "I'm going to change my priorities right here." From that time on, through my life thus far, I have put Ted first and then my children second. I think that's what God wants: God first; our mate second; and then the children. The Lord has honored this over the years.

Then God put another love in orbit for us. Billy Graham had come to Grand Rapids, and Ted helped to organize Billy's first

Crusade. Well, there had been a doctor and his wife up in Northern Michigan who had had such a rough life and had just recently become Christians. They wanted to come down to Grand Rapids to hear Billy Graham at that Crusade. They got to meet Billy and became good friends. After one of the meetings, we had everybody to our house, Billy and the team and all, for coffee and late supper. The doctor and his wife came along, too. They soon realized that we wanted another baby and the doctor said, "Okay, I know of one on the way, and you will be first on the list." So, through him, we got our beautiful Don.

Was there any problem explaining to the children that they were adopted?

None. We'd been open with them from the beginning. We shared with them all these fun stories as they grew up, so they understood how blessed and privileged we all were.

Anyhow, getting back to Don, we brought him home. We lived on a block with thirty-two children. When I was in the kitchen, having lunch with my mom and dad who were there helping me a bit, the baby was asleep in his little basket. Gordon, three years old then, came in and took the baby out of the basket and put him over his left arm. He opened the front door and went out on the porch, intending to show the other kids in the neighborhood our new addition. They had all been anxious to see him, and Gordon wanted to show him off. I discovered what was going on just as he was heading down those steps. I couldn't scream or yell or anything because this would startle Gordon, and he'd drop the baby. But I managed to get him to turn around. We all had a good laugh later. At the time, though, it was kind of tense.

Did you adopt any other children?

Yes, we did. We lived right across the street from Pat and Mary Zondervan. We could share so much of what we felt about life, what with both couples having adopted children.

At one point I told Mary, after she and Pat had adopted a baby girl, "Oh, Mary, we want a baby girl so much." She said, "Here is a telephone number in Louisville, Kentucky. By next year you'll have your daughter." So that's exactly what happened. On our way to Florida that winter, for a YFC convention, we stopped in Louisville and had an interview. While in Florida we received a call from the home in Louisville, and, on the way home, we stopped in to pick up our baby girl. Her daddy named her JoAnn.

Our two guys, Gordon and Donny, had just gotten over the chicken pox. They were in the back of the station wagon because they couldn't go into the home. The lady at the home followed us outside to meet the boys. She chatted with them and got great big smiles and all. Then I had another "apple pie" story, because she wrote on the application, "I was so impressed by the patches on their blue jeans, I decided any mother that can patch blue jeans that neatly will make a *wonderful* mother."

The funny part was that our kids were so active that they would go through the knees, and we were using already made patches that I ironed on! She had not seen these.

As we continued home, we stopped at a restaurant. The baby was in a basket off to one side with these two darling little boys leaning over her, just adoring her. The people in the restaurant couldn't get over little brothers so taken by a baby. They didn't know she was brand new.

Some couples feel, today, that it's better not to have any children, that it's too much of a responsibility. How would you respond?

Yes, that's the way of so much of the world these days. But there just wouldn't have been as much joy in our marriage if there had not been children. I enjoy them so very much. They're all close by, and we have three darling grandchildren. The rewards of all those years now are just coming back to give us great joy.

Ruth Graham

Few people on earth could have more of a treasure chest of memories than Ruth Graham—she has been to practically every worthwhile spot on the globe; met with presidents, royalty, prime ministers; traveled by rickshaw, donkey, car, boat, and plane. There have been nights when going to bed and then having to wake up an hour or so later have been harder than simply *not* sleeping at all.

"God never said the role of a mother, a wife, would be an easy one," Ruth was saying as we sat on the front porch of their home at Montreat, North Carolina. "The marriage vows suggest this . . . *richer or poorer, sickness or health* . . . and marriage should never be embarked upon with the notion that it's all glorious. Nor should motherhood. A great deal of plain hard work, sometimes frustration, become part and parcel of a woman's life. But the role shouldn't be avoided because the tasks at times seem tough."

"What are the most severe problems you have had as a mother?" I asked at this point.

"I worried, at the beginning, about Bill being away from home so much. I always thought a father had to be around much more than he was able to be. On occasion I felt sorry for the children not having a 'normal' home. Yet I had the feeling, the confidence really, that since God had called Bill to this ministry He would make up the lack. He would make it all up to the children. God was—and I mean this very reverently—honor bound to do this. I would do whatever I could to hold up my end of the bargain. The rest was God's responsibility."

We sat quietly for a few minutes, enjoying the clean air, the coolness as it tapped gently on our faces. I was impressed with Ruth. Someone who should have known better wasn't awfully sure how candid Ruth would be on a variety of subjects. She was accustomed to waiting in the wings, so to speak, while Billy held center stage, calling her out only from time to time.

But Ruth had her own life, too. With Billy being away so much, she always found it necessary to "shift for herself." This is one of the strong underpinnings of their marriage. The old cliche of absence making the heart grow fonder really is accurate in their case, utterly demolishing any insinuations of marital difficulty.

"Your husband seems to many of us to be a really extraordinary man," I said honestly. "Has he always had a certain *charisma* about him?"

"When he was just a young man, I'd have to say that the answer was no. He had tremendous drive and energy, but he was not a brilliant student. He worked hard on the farm as he was growing up, but he was not an exceptional athlete. There was absolutely nothing you might say was exceptional about him, which is a good thing, actually. It showed that God in His sovereignty could reach down and pick up an ordinary person, and make someone useful of that person. Useful, that is, for the purpose of spreading the 'Good News' in a significant way.

"Bill wasn't born with any exceptional gifts. He had to develop, just like most people. His speaking style at the beginning was not what it is today. He was just in the early stages of his ministry; he was a real shouter in those days. Sometimes, what with my Presbyterian background, I just wasn't so sure of him, and at times, because he talked so fast, I couldn't even understand what he said. Now he's slowed down considerably and talks more slowly and distinctly.

"You know," she said, "there are so many people today who

need help. They're caught in one sort of net or another. But they don't seem to be able to come to that point where they turn over *everything* to the Lord and let Him assume command. He may be their Savior, but He's not as yet Lord of their lives.

"What they have to do is come to Christ and say, 'Lord, I need help.' Suppose it's drug addiction or alcoholism or something sexual or selfishness or a hot temper or love of gossip. These are the areas that seem to be afflicting folks with such severity today. After talking to other mothers, as well as young people, I see how pervasive the anguish, the entrapment continues to be.

"People caught in a sin must be sorry enough to *want* to quit. That's what repentance is all about. It's the Holy Spirit who makes us unhappy with our own sinful condition and actions, and we must appeal to Him for His supernatural help."

"Prayer is a crucial part of a change in a person's life. Isn't that so, Ruth?"

"That's right."

"I have a problem with my own prayer life," I admitted. "I have a long list of people to pray for. I don't keep in touch with most of them on a regular basis, so I don't know if the matter in prayer has been resolved one way or the other. So it's the same people, the same needs, night after night, long stretch after long stretch, sometimes years. Human nature being what it is, you can become bored and restless through the sheer act of repetition, a certain sameness creeping in. How is that to be avoided, particularly if those needs these people have continue to be felt?"

She thought for a moment, then answered, "I think there's such a thing as committing it all to our Lord, whether an individual or a situation. When you do that you leave whatever or whomever it is there with Him—and let it go for the Lord to handle.

"In my case, for example, there's just no way I could daily pray for everyone who's on my heart. But, as situations arise, when I know there's a real need, then they're the ones who are uppermost in my prayers. I've committed so many people to the Lord over the years, saying, 'Lord, You have a place for them, a purpose. Do what You need to do in their lives.'

"It's interesting, years later, when I pull out old prayer lists and consider what has happened to the individuals concerned. I see how the Lord has answered prayers which I had frankly forgotten, due to the passage of time.

17

"I remember one such instance: I was growing up in China. We had a man working for us who had run away from the army years before. Finally they caught him, and as punishment they cut off his ears. So he wore his hair like a girl's, with bangs and hair down over his ears.

"He was a great tease, and, occasionally, for a special treat, he would let us see where his ears had been. But he was not a Christian, and this concerned us considerably. When I went to high school he was still in my prayers, and I did pray for him earnestly. But then over the years other needs came into my prayers. I guess I just committed him to the Lord, and forgot.

"A long time later I learned that after he had left the employ of Mother and Daddy he joined the bandits. You see, we lived in the middle of bandit territory. They sometimes were respected businessmen by day but at night became bandits. Our friend had been captured later and put in prison. While there an evangelist visited the prisoners, and brought him to Christ that way. Though I had forgotten to pray, the Lord hadn't forgotten."

Ruth smiled and added, "I think a busy wife and mother understands better than anyone else what Paul meant when he wrote that we were to pray without ceasing. Because if you had to be on your knees and locked in a closet when you prayed, a busy wife and mother would have very little time, if any, to pray in the 'accepted' manner.

"I know some who do get up early and spend two or three hours at a stretch in prayer, but we have had five children. The first four were abominable sleepers, meaning I would have to get up anywhere from one to seven times a night. Consequently there was no such thing as regular hours during those years. It would have done no one any good if I had collapsed from exhaustion!

"I'll admit, though, that not praying according to a regular schedule did bother me. And then I realized the significance of what Paul said. I realized that a mother can pray on her feet. She can pray while she's making beds, while she's dusting, while she's driving a car, while she's shopping. Prayer for me has never been just at a set time of day or night. It's a continual conversation with God. You carry on a conversation all day long. Still, when possible, early morning is my favorite time for Bible study and prayer."

"Have there been times when your burdens as a mother, a wife, were so great that you wondered what to do?" I asked.

18

"Frequently, yes. When the burdens have gotten that heavy as a result of some particular situation or individual, then I've been literally driven to prayer but, also, to the Word of God. And when I read His Word, I receive greater strength from 'listening' to what He says to me than what I have to say to Him."

"Now, your husband is not considered 'intellectual,' and he is scoffed at by some intellectuals as a result. Does this ever make him feel inadequate?"

"Yes, many times he has said he would love to return to college, would love to go on to a seminary. But I think it is just as well he hasn't, because I think a sense of inadequacy can often be a great advantage. It makes you work all the harder."

We interrupted the interview so that I could snap some pictures. Ruth posed with the grace of a professional model. Having been the object of so many camera lenses over the years, she knew exactly what contributed to good photographs.

"If your husband were to become 'more intellectual,' as it were," I continued, "what greater insight could he have or what greater value could he be to the Lord than he has been already?"

"I think his ministry is primarily to the ordinary man on the street. To be able to explain the gospel simply so that a little child can understand it, well, that's a gift. I've watched the interest audiences betray when he's speaking. The smallest child seems to be listening as attentively as the adults. Both his written ministry and his speaking ministry are to average people. Thank God there are already others appealing to the intellectuals."

I hesitated with the final question of the interview. Christians should not be guided by gossip, rumor. So I asked, with the greatest trepidation, about some reports of which I'd recently been made aware.

"Ruth, it seems to be a subject of conversation that Billy has been talking and/or thinking a lot about death lately. There is suspicion that he has perhaps had a premonition and feels he doesn't have an exceptionally long amount of time left."

"I know one man who expected to die for over fifty years. But seriously, I think he's being realistic. He had a heart attack some time ago. But he didn't realize it at the time. If his doctors had been made aware of it, they would have put him in the hospital. He's a driver, you know. He forces himself a lot. He runs two miles a day when I think he should be walking instead. He has had other health problems. He's not getting any younger. He's into his sixties now, and yet he's still working as hard or harder than when he was considerably younger.

"I would love to see him slow down. Actually, sometimes Christians take advantage of him and pressure him into commitments. He's obligated to so many people that it's hard to say no. They press him into doing things which he was not called of God to do. He was called to proclaim the gospel to the unconverted, and that is his gift. It's communicating the gospel, not dedicating buildings or preaching funerals or even performing wedding ceremonies. That's why I've said, quite seriously, that if I should die before he does, and he's halfway around the world, the burial arrangements should go on without delay, because his place is where the Lord would have him to be, performing the Great Commission. There's no way you could just drop a crusade and fly home. He could lay some flowers on my grave when he got home."

She paused, then concluded, "We're as happy today as when we were first married, frankly. Actually, much happier. We've learned to deal with the problems. For example, a great many wives and mothers have asked me about how I dealt with the loneliness, the separations. For one thing, I said, I seldom had time to be lonely with five kids. I was blessed because, during the early years, we lived across the street from my father and my mother, until we moved up here. Daddy was a father figure to the children, and we were extremely blessed by having them. They not only were godly but they were fun to be with, absolutely delightful. They read to the children, played games with them. Daddy was also a doctor. We were spoiled because we had our own house physician.

"I think that what needs to be said is that no one, not even a husband, no matter how deeply he is loved, can take the place of the Lord Jesus Christ. I really feel that we women who call ourselves Christians need to draw on the Lord Jesus for all He has to offer to us, so we can be free to be the wives our husbands need and the mothers our children require. For instance, in the average home, the wife works hard, with no household help, and she has to do the shopping, the cleaning, the laundry, the cooking, you name it. Then when her husband comes home at night she spills all her frustrations and complaints and problems with the children and whatever else on his shoulders."

"And he in turn has had problems at the office."

"That's right. He's been working under much tension, pressure, frustration himself. The inevitable result is that there is a clash and, if he's not a committed Christian, real trouble can develop.

"But if the wife takes each problem as it arises to the Lord in prayer, if there is a personal relationship with Christ, these problems have been dealt with by evening and she is free to listen to *his* problems. She's ready to love him, be cheerful, just *be* his wife. So that is what is meant in the Bible when it talks about the marital relationship. The husband should love his wife as Christ loved the church and gave himself for it. Neither is doing that when they let their problems blow up in their faces without going to the Lord in prayerful conversation as they should, searching the Scriptures for answers and applying them to life.

"We learn everything we need to know about life from the Bible. We should apply its teachings to every aspect of our daily existence. If we do, the family unit will remain strong. If we don't, all the forces seeking to tear it apart will be successful."

Today, Ruth seems to have a well-grounded faith. She is the epitome of a solid Christian wife and mother. But was she always this way, devoted to Christ without question?

"There was a time when I had serious doubts," Ruth admitted. "You see, I had a friend with whom I had gone to school in Korea. Over the years we were separated and lost contact with one another. Then, later, when I was a student at Wheaton College, this friend was at the University of Chicago. He came down to visit with some of his old high-school friends.

"I found out that he had lost his faith there at the University. The professor in question was so outspoken that he warned the class from the outset, 'If any of you are believing Christians now, you will leave my class with your faith destroyed.'

"My friend told me that there was a girl who had an even stronger faith than he did, and she became an avowed atheist. He was quick to point out that he hadn't gone that far, that he was merely an agnostic. He then said, 'Ruth, you ought to lose your faith. It would do you a world of good.'

"Well, I had never had anybody say that to me before, and it shook me up. I began to question. If it's not possible to believe that the Bible is the Word of God—if that goes—how can you believe that Jesus is the Son of God or that we have salvation through His atoning death?

21

"I used to argue the various points with just about everybody. Friends used to dread seeing me come into the dining hall. 'Oh, here comes Ruth,' they'd whisper.'We'll have another argument.'

"They didn't know that I wasn't arguing to win—I was arguing to lose. This has been a great lesson down through the years, when I come across people who are very argumentative. I keep saying in the back of my mind, 'Maybe they are not arguing to win, maybe they are arguing to lose, hoping that someone will come up with hard facts that will absolutely pulverize their theories.'

"At this time I was going with one of the more brilliant students on campus—he was a senior and I was a freshman. He sensed that something was wrong. And right off he said, 'You're having trouble with your faith, aren't you?' I replied, 'You can say that again.' He wanted to take me to different professors on campus, but I knew exactly what would happen. They might get emotional, I thought, and say, 'Let's pray about it, Ruth,' so I said no. 'I don't want emotion. I want cold, hard facts.' He started giving these to me, arguing in a very sensible way, stating points that I'd never heard expressed so concisely, so lucidly.

"And he concluded simply, but unexpectedly, 'Ruth, there is still the leap of faith.' And I understood. Because if everything were solely on an intellectual plane, then only the brightest people, the educated ones could come to know Him. But God has chosen to reveal himself through childlike faith. In this way little children, the mentally retarded can come to know Him, personally. And the genius has to come as a little child, by faith."

"Is it, ultimately, so bad, then, to have your faith tested so long as you regain it in an even stronger form than previously?"

"I can't say that it is or isn't good as a general rule. I just know what happened in my own personal instance. I read somewhere about a young man who went to see an abnormally saintly bishop and confessed that he was losing his faith. The bishop replied, 'No, son, you are just losing your parents' faith. Go out now and get one of your own.'

"That's what happened to me, of course. I had accepted on face value what I had been taught as a child, but that had had to be translated into something I could accept on my own. Since then my faith has never waned, not in the slightest."

"If I came to you as a confirmed, lifelong atheist," I proposed, "how would you go about converting me?"

22

"I would say that you were the biggest gambler on earth. It takes more faith, of a sort, to be an atheist than it does to be a Christian. You see, if I—as a Christian—am wrong, I've lost nothing. I have had unspeakable joy and peace during this life, even through difficult situations. I have had the comfort, the instruction, the guidance found in the Bible. Even if it all were a hoax, I have lost nothing. Whereas the atheist has lost a terrible gamble if *he's* proven wrong."

Joan Winmill Brown

Oh, the joy that fills my soul. . . .

Those words from a popular Christian song are being repeated often.

Oh, the joy. . . .

Just *thinking* them is supposed to banish the melancholy from our lives.

Oh . . .

But it's seldom that easy. After years of despair, layer upon layer of one kind of mean, sorrowful, depressing circumstance after another, saying/thinking a few cheerful words can be more hollow than revitalizing, can worsen what is supposed to be alleviated.

Nothing as trite and convenient can save you from swallowing a fatal dose of pills or sticking your head into a gas oven.

Nothing. . . .

Many years later, an ocean of trauma later, when you have your husband and your sons by your side, especially at Christmastime, you realize with a mixture of regret and gratitude what the journey to this time, this place entailed. . . .

Are your sons today as unhurting as you would like them to be? I mean, do they have any emotional sores as you did? Or have they been relatively fortunate in this respect?

I don't think there is anybody these days who doesn't have a hurt of some sort. I mean you can put on a big front. Bill Jr. is a policeman/paramedic. To meet him you wouldn't think he had any problems at all, and yet I'm sure, as a result of his work, he sees many tragedies. He was a paramedic before he was a policeman, and he seemed to age ten years. He was only nineteen when he started. He's seen so much death. But when you have the faith we have in this family, you do go on until the next time, and then the time after that. Spiritual faith helps tremendously.

David has been going through the problems that all teenagers do . . . not quite sure where he's going in life, making hard decisions. There are so many pressures in general these days.

Have you found, as a result of circumstances in your childhood, that it has been rougher or easier for you as a mother?

I haven't had any kind of permanent home to base experience or comparison on, you see. However, I think maybe it's made me a little more understanding of the insecurities common to people, young or old. I've really asked the Lord to give wisdom in full measure, what with David and Bill Jr. having such different personalities, and the need to understand them both. In a sense I'm grateful that I had the kind of background I did, because I can relate to people so much better now. But, no, I can never claim it's been ideal.

Would you say that you are a strong person today as a result of your childhood years, and the success of your battles against traumas encountered then and since?

Through the Lord, yes. I know I couldn't do anything without Him. I think basically I'm the same emotionally weak person that I was, but with His strength, well, that's all changed. I can do all things through Christ, who strengthens me.

Did your sons know about your childhood before your book and then the film came out?

25

I would say that *No Longer Alone* revealed everything to them more vividly than any clues I might have provided otherwise. I was very concerned about how they would react. I worried that they might be embarrassed in some way.

When the boys saw the film, it was David who said, "I know it's going to help a lot of people, Mom."

"You don't mind?" I asked him.

"No, not at all," he replied. "I love you—and I'm glad everything's better now for you."

It's interesting that David has only one friend, I think, who has his original parents. Nearly all the others have been divorced. And that's hard, really, because you look at them and wonder if the same thing is ever going to happen in your own family. It's like waiting for a hidden time bomb to explode, I suppose.

Now, since you were an only child, and talk from experience, especially in view of the background you've had, have you often had to confront the personal obstacle of feeling terribly, terribly inadequate as you went through life?

Most of the time, frankly. I never felt I belonged anywhere—with anyone. I always sensed that I was on the sidelines, waiting to join in but never doing it. Even after accepting Christ into my life, such feelings lingered. My husband Bill has helped quite a bit. But it's like learning to live your life all over again. In those days the theater tended to become the image I responded to—because I never had had a mother image. And that, of course, only added to my problems, the theater being what it is.

Interestingly enough—though I know that Protestants often don't like to be in a position that appears to revere the name of Mary—Mary was an example that did help me much, during those early years and later. For instance, when I knew I was expecting Bill Jr. and then David, I had to travel a lot, and I thought of what Mary had to suffer during her pregnancy, with none of the modern conveniences. She never complained, so far as we can tell.

Over the years I've read more and more into Mary. And I think about how she had to learn to let go of her very special Son. That showed me that *every* mother comes to a place where she has to say hands off and give her children their independence. Otherwise they are never going to be able to cope with life. You have to let them make their own mistakes, and that's very hard for a mother to comprehend at first. I wish I could be around always, saving them from any kind of hurt, whether they fall physically or emotionally or whatever. I'm sure Mary must have prayed and agonized many times in this way about Jesus. The agony she must have gone through as she stood at the cross!

Are young people a special target of Satan today, in your opinion?

Definitely yes. Satan is trying very hard to subvert them through drugs and all the rest. I think we have to be much more on the alert, not so complacent. Living these days is full of promise, I'll admit, but also full of potential disaster.

Along with the attack upon children has come an attack upon motherhood itself—the role of the wife in the home. Would you care to comment on this apparent trend?

I remember when the children were quite young. We were living in Columbus, Ohio. Bill would fly all over the place and come back and be there to help with the children when they got measles and chicken pox and what-have-you. But then he had to leave again. And, invariably, that was when everything really went wrong. You name it—broken down washing machines, everything else, it seemed—it all went to pot. Not while Bill was home, but after he left the house!

I used to feel kind of sorry for myself but, in retrospect, I realize I had the wonderful joy of spending those days with my children. The other day I said something to Bill about an incident that happened involving David. He said that he didn't remember that one. Or I talk about something else, and Bill doesn't remember that, either. Then he admits that he doesn't recall very much about the children when they were young. So, in a sense, I really did have the better part of it, because I was gathering memories.

I think the trouble is that the glossy magazines and films and TV shows make a mother's role look mundane, very unimportant, something to rebel against.

I like to think of family life as a huge jigsaw puzzle; each day you put in another piece. It's like this, in my opinion, especially with a child's life in the very early years of your relationship with him. At some point you come close to that final piece, and it is then when you know or at least catch a glimmer of whether you've done the job of raising him well or you've done it poorly.

Certainly the time for that final piece hasn't come as yet in my boys' lives—perhaps it never will. You see, I realize that the greatest act a mother can perform is to pray for her children, and it seems to me that this is virtually a never-ending requirement.

What are the special frustrations, as you see them, peculiar to being a mother?

I think, before a child comes into the world at birth, that we all tend to expect so much of him. We want to put him into a mold, rather like making a little robot really. You have to realize, though, and the sooner the better, that that child is his own being. You can do your best to guide that child but you cannot dominate him for the rest of his life. Regardless of what happens, it's so important to be philosophical, to keep a sense of humor, particularly on those frequent days when everything does seem to go wrong.

Furthermore, I shouldn't fail to mention that I could never get through the day without constantly being in touch with the Lord. Every time the boys left to go to school, I always prayed for them. I pray for Bill Jr. as he works, for David as his own world gets larger and larger.

You know, I feel so very privileged to be a mother. I never wanted to be a mother a long time ago. That may sound strange, contradictory to many people, but my own mother died in childbirth, so I was terrified of that word. Childbirth and its implications, at least as far as I was concerned, were not for me. Maybe I'd adopt a couple of children one day, but that was all.

When I was pregnant with Bill Jr., tremendous fears swept through me. But I prayed earnestly, and asked the Lord to help me and He really did. I knew, more strongly than ever, that He was with me, and once again it was the example of Mary that served to help me.

Were those fears because you felt you'd die as a result of childbirth, or were they because you questioned your own competence as a mother because of the childhood you'd experienced?

I think it was both. Having been an actress I had never known what it was to be disciplined on a daily basis. I'd be in a show and you'd have to be disciplined then. But I knew that, sooner or later, that show was coming to an end and I'd have different hours, a different part, wouldn't have to get up at a certain set time, and so on. The role of being a mother was difficult for me, but the wonderful thing is that the Lord being in your life changes you, your whole outlook. I know that making beds used to get me down, until I realized that that was a wonderful time to pray. You were making that bed for someone, so you could use the time to pray for that person.

I did the same with ironing. If you're ironing your husband's shirt, pray for him at that time, think of him lovingly.

So many mothers make a god out of tidiness. Ruth Graham helped me so much with that. She said that communication is the most important thing you can have with your child. A tidy room is not the most important, especially if it impedes communication and causes a fuss out of all proportion to the situation.

I can remember when my boys hit their teens. Well, there were times they were very unlovely in their behavior, but I realized this was when they needed me the most. I wouldn't condone their behavior, but I would say, by word and deed, in the midst of it all, that I still loved them. I knew what they were going through.

And this attitude on my part seemed to help them so much. I knew that the times I was the most unlovely was when I needed love the most. How unlovely I must have been to the Lord, and yet He loved me in spite of it all.

What impact does it have on families when teenagers go to jail? Do most parents reject them? Do they say, in effect, "I'm so embarrassed—what will I say to my friends?" Or do they react with real love and sympathy?

I've found it works both ways. Parents so often cry and wail and are desperately hurt. They don't want to have anything to do with the young person. I get so many letters from people who are in prison and find that nobody else writes to them or seems to care about them. I try to point out that the Lord doesn't reject them.

It's sad, really. They apparently don't have a friend in the world. They are asking me to be their friend. And I think to myself, "Where are their parents?"

I remember one particular case. I had not communicated with this person but had read about him, and seen him on television. He's the child of a very well-known family. Yet they hardly ever write to him—really such a tragedy. It is like this with this one young man and many, many others. Basically we all love to brag about our successes, but life isn't always filled with successes. I think we have to be very honest. While that child is in prison, he will hope, more than anything, that someone outside does care. Otherwise there's nothing to live for, and he invariably becomes worse as a result.

I do a lot of prison visitation. I see them sitting there, with a big facade around them, acting as though it doesn't bother them, but deep down inside they're lonely, desperate.

I am convinced that cynicism and such could be cut way down if Christians would do more work in prisons.

Have you come across many instances of child abuse, be it physical or emotional?

It's always a tremendous problem. I've counseled prisoners who have had a terribly unhappy childhood because of emotional deprivation as well as physical attacks by one or both parents.

I try to get them not to dwell on this, to turn the defeats, the pain, into victories for the Lord. That's the key, you know. Whenever we engage in sin, displease the Lord, the human tendency is to dwell on it and feel very guilty about it and allow our behavior, our outlook, to be affected drastically. It's not that we should become flippant or nonchalant about sin and, as some groups do, confess and then go on to commit sin again and again. This makes confession and pseudo-repentance very mechanical, very artificial and shallow. We *should* feel *deeply* about sin, abhor it in fact. My conviction, however, is that guilt is the devil's tool, compounding the sin. We're told that the Lord is faithful and just and forgives us all our sins and cleanses us from all unrighteousness. But when we profess that promise, yet don't apply it in reality, we really are being hypocritical.

Macel Falwell

Not compromising is tough. Today's society is one, seemingly, almost suicidally bent on compromise. Moral causes are side-stepped in favor of pragmatic answers. The Pilgrims and Puritans of centuries ago would have cried in utter despair at the mess made of the "New Israel" that was their intended direction for America.

These influences—the immoral, the pragmatic—are of constant concern to Jerry Falwell. As a prominent preacher on Sunday television stations each week, Jerry is continually approached through letters, phone calls, and personal visits from viewers of *The Old Time Gospel Hour* who want him to know that they share his concern.

The potential problems, domestically, don't require a Sherlock Holmes to discern. But *potential* is all that they seem to be. Macel, Jerry's wife, and he have been very successful over the years at maintaining the private part of their lives that is indispensable to the stability of the family.

"You keep pretty much in the background, don't you?" I asked as Macel, Jerry, and I sat in a secluded spot of a Lynchburg restaurant on a cold, windy, snowy Saturday evening.

"I feel I've been called to be Jerry's wife, and the mother of his children, and not to be in the spotlight," she said, smiling a bit. "It's Jerry's ministry. While I share in it with him, and support him every step of the way, I think he is the one God has chosen. As his wife I should conduct myself exactly as I have been doing all these years. Besides, the children need me. I spend most of my time with them. I became convinced a long time ago that I can do a better job if I sort of stay in the background."

She paused for a moment, then added: "I want the children to know that Jerry and I are interested in everything they do, ready to help them at a moment's notice. One or both of us is around, regardless of the hour or the day. They never have to wonder where we are. If it's a football game, we go with them. If it's something else, we share that, too. A family in the Biblical sense is a tight, close unit. With so much in the world that is opposed to the family, Jerry and I are so careful to go in the opposite direction, and keep our family together.

"I remember one time when Jonathan, our youngest son, had a birthday party. Jerry was supposed to have been at some special meeting. So, knowing what an important day it was for his son, he approached Jonathan and said, 'Son, I can do one of two things: I can cancel my participation in this meeting and let someone else go for me, or I can give you my honorarium when I get back.' (Laughter) Jonathan replied, 'I'd rather have you.' So Jerry sent someone in his place. I think it's crucial to the children to know that we care enough to cancel a meeting or rearrange our plans in other ways if this is important enough in their eyes."

As a preacher's wife, Macel, what personal problems do people ask you about?"

"Oh, there's certainly a variety," she said. "I remember that one was about a lady wearing pantsuits! (Laughter) Several preachers' wives have written asking about problems in their churches and how to handle these: How they should dress, questions about makeup, dating behavior, and so on. Mostly the wives are the younger ones, new to the responsibilities involved, and they need guidance. They ask me how I would handle myself."

"As a pastor's wife, the mother of three P. K.'s, do you occasionally feel isolated from members of the congregation because

32

of the truism that you can't become friendly with one or two members at the risk of being accused of favoritism?''

"I don't seem to encounter any of that. Most of my very closest friends in the Thomas Road congregation and I have been together since we were in high school. There's not been any criticism of which I am aware. We all were raised up together here, part of the same small town way of life. I know I'm fortunate, we all are, because it has been a problem in other churches.

"I suppose I've always had the idea that I am going to be criticized constantly *whatever* I do. So I decided years ago to seek the Lord's will. Once I'm convinced I'm following Him, as He wants, then I'm happy irrespective of even the harshest criticism.''

"Traditionally, Macel, pastors' kids have supposedly had severe emotional and spiritual problems, more so than 'ordinary' kids. Is that true in your family? Does the congregation look to your youngsters and expect them to conduct themselves differently?''

"I don't think so. Our children seem to be just as average as anyone's in the ministry. They don't attract special favoritism or attention at all. If anything, I am told that our kids act less like P.K.'s than is generally the rule. Somebody asked Jeannie what it was like to be the child of a famous man. She replied, 'Famous, what do you mean? Somebody else in our church owns a McDonald's!' In her mind that's just as special as her dad being on TV and all the rest.''

One of the worst pressures for Macel was Jerry's encounter with the Securities and Exchange Commission several years ago. Much publicity swirled around this, and many outsiders looked with suspicion upon the ministry, even though everything was eventually cleared up.

"That was really the hardest," Macel continued. "When I went shopping, I kept thinking that all those people thought that my husband had done something wrong. It was very difficult until the press publicized the outcome, which set the record straight.''

"When we won the case," Jerry added, "it all just took a complete turnaround. People are like that. You can be a hero today, a heel tomorrow, then back to being a hero again. You've got to realize that this is part of your life if you want to be where you are. But, you know, this ordeal succeeded in bringing our family much closer together.''

Right now this family is happy. Right now everything is going well. But right now the children are yet living within the family circle. Another world awaits them when they leave home. So many parents find what they felt about their youngsters to be almost illusionary, once sons and daughters go out into the world. Perceptions are altered and morality plummets.

"Does this concern you, Macel? As a mother, do you ever wonder if your astuteness in raising them will be the 'guarantee' they need when they face life beyond the home?"

"Well, I would be really surprised if they went off the track. It's important that they know they are loved, no matter what. If there are problems, they can come to us without hesitation. They do this now—all the time, asking advice, whatever. We include the children in everything. We never even think about activities without their being a part."

"According to an article in your newspaper, The Journal-American, if your children are late from time to time you get panicky. Why panicky? Is that an accurate word?"

"I just really like to know where they are every minute. If they are supposed to be back at a certain time, I want them back at that time. Even when they go on trips, like field trips for school. If they're due back at 10:30, then at 10:45 I'm looking for them." (Laughter)

"And if it's a significant amount of time that has lapsed, it's going to have to be accounted for," Jerry put in.

"We get on the telephone and call around asking, 'Do you know where they are?' " Macel said. "Both of us are very sensitive about this."

"Here's an interesting point," I said. "You're not going to be worried about how they act after they leave home and begin lives apart from the close family circle, but you're panicky if they're even a few minutes late now. Isn't that a contradiction?"

"Perhaps it is. But I just feel better when I know what's happening. We never achieve total consistency this side of glory."

"Someone who feels the way you do, if it weren't for your natural common sense and the Lord's leading, could tip over from being a mother into being also a dictator. How do you avoid crossing the thin line I'm talking about?"

"Yes, I'm aware of that thin line. I'm always trying to guard against tipping over, as you say, because, you see, my own mother was like that. So I guess I get this tendency from her. I try to pull

34

back when the danger signs are there."

"Rigidity, though it is necessary," Jerry added, "must be tempered with an overdose of love. Our kids feel very loved, but also very much under authority."

It was getting late. Jerry had three church services to shepherd the next morning. Macel and he dropped me off at the motel where I was staying, indicating that someone would pick me up to take me to church.

Back at the motel I happened to see a cover line on one of the risque magazines proliferating at newsstands everywhere. The daughter of a major Christian celebrity had given an interview to that publication. Her testimony in print came across strongly enough, but across from the last part of the interview were color photos of . . . well, no need to depict what was involved. Suffice it to say that the shots were obscene and gross.

I began asking myself a hard question: Could her parents have been happy? Glad that she gave her testimony so strongly, yes—but were they delighted with the *forum*?

I determined to put the question to Macel after church. . . .

When we went out for lunch after the service, I had the opportunity to ask:

"Let's say you have a child who comes to you and says, 'Mom, I have this tremendous chance to give my testimony in this nudie-type magazine. It can reach hundreds of thousands of people for the Lord who would not ordinarily encounter the gospel in such a way. Would you let me do it?' How would you approach that issue, Macel?"

"I would advise my child not to do it. I think it would hurt my child's reputation. I think it would hurt the cause of Christ. I don't think anything like that is necessary."

"I agree with you, Macel," I said honestly. "But, looking at it from another point of view, one could possibly say, 'Well, that type of person, the one who reads such magazines, needs to encounter more witnessing than those who read the cleaner publications. How else can we reach him?' "

"A verse of Scripture that comes to mind," Jerry interposed, "is the one that says, 'Don't cast your pearls before swine.' The rationale that allows you to become involved with such a magazine can allow you to go into a disco place to 'help' the people there. The same rationale would permit me to go into a massage parlor and witness to everybody coming in and going out. I don't think you have to use that platform. You can somehow reach those people without compromising your personal code of ethics."

"Jerry, one report recently said that seventy-five percent of all young people are interested and/or involved in religion, that religion is an important part of life for them. But at the same time we apparently have a rise in teenage suicide. Isn't there a contradiction in such seeming antithetical stories?"

"I think a lot of that religious interest is in the mystical, the Eastern religions. It's not a genuine Christian perspective. They don't find all that they're looking for, so they try suicide. Furthermore, the situation is not being helped by weak parents who breed weak teenagers. Without the anchor of Christ in their lives, they feel they have no place to turn but to the act of committing suicide."

That evening, once again after church, the three of us got together again. It had been a good day, a day of worship, uplifting music, and fellowship that was blessed. Our lives merged, briefly, and we shared thoughts about many subjects.

One of these was the nature of love. A mother loves her children in a special way. Then one day those children leave her and set up homes of their own because of another sort of love that has entered *their* world.

At least that's how it should be. The intimacies that come as a result of marriage force a man and a woman together in more than the physical ways. They become as one emotionally, even spiritually, and they can stand against the world and all of its encroachments. But they also must realize that the hard times, in whatever form, are not merely *likely* to come but are in fact *destined* to do so. The heartache will be there, sooner or later. It may be so very intense, so very all pervasive, that only the enablement of God's Holy Spirit and their devotion to one another will cause them to survive. Be it cancer, the death of a family member, financial disaster, whatever, they must face something in life that intrudes upon their little "Eden" of intimacy.

If the worldly view of marriage is not, at the one extreme, vulgar and degraded, it is, at the other, so highly romanticized that young people enter into it expecting the proverbial bed of roses to be what will face them in years hence. After all, everything does end happily, isn't that true?

Not usually . . . in this life, anyway.

For a vast number of couples, the happy ending must wait until they meet again in Heaven. Their earthly lives are ripped by so much heartache as to eclipse the patent and vulgar phoniness of TV and movie fiction.

"That *is* a problem," Macel acknowledged, her expression serious. "After twenty years plus in a growing ministry, I have heard the best as well as the worst of life's experiences."

There have been personal dramas of death and paralysis; the loss of arms or legs; people have gone blind, become deaf, lost their sanity; senility has transported once brilliant minds into a gloomy twilight world of increasing incapacitation.

We'd been talking about the romanticizing of love that is propagated by lyrical musical ballads and mushy romance novels.

"The reality doesn't catch up to the dream," Macel said. "Couples become disillusioned as a result. They expect it all to be more exciting, and disappointment sets in. They become disappointed with one another instead of realizing that the romantic myths are partially what is at fault."

Macel and Jerry are trying hard to steer a middle ground in terms of how they approach parenthood, setting the right example for their children: In essence, don't expect too little or too much from life. When you get married, commit that relationship to the Lord.

I left Lynchburg the next morning. The weather was not good. A cold, cold wind was blowing, whipping up clouds of snow from huge mounds piled everywhere. More bad wintry conditions were being forecast. I would eventually be heading back to California to warmer weather. The thought was appealing to say the least.

Even so, I lingered until the last moment. My moments with the Falwells revealed a special part of their lives—after the TV cameras have been switched off, and the congregation has left the sanctuary. There are a few, sometimes very few, moments of free time like this. In this precious time, Macel and Jerry and the three children will go home and relax and thank God for one another.

Doris Moody

The Pressures of Being Pastor's Kids

As Dr. Jess Moody's wife, I've seen these for a long time now. My son and my daughter have been through a great deal. As the children of a well-known Baptist minister, they've been forced to try and fill the role of model young people. We were supposed to have the model family in all respects, else how could my husband preach solutions to others?

That's the basic problem of having a pastor as a father, a husband. People go to him with their problems, and he's either not supposed to have any or he's supposed to be able to solve them easily. But to whom does he go with his difficulties? Or to whom do other members of the family go? They must keep the frustrations, the tribulations common to man within the family circle, and not let the outside world get a peek.

But on no members of the family is all this harder than on the youngsters. One of our kids adjusted pretty well, the other did not. Yet both had the same environment. I guess our daughter is more like her father, more resilient, while our son is a bit more like me. I have a difficult time adjusting to pressure situations.

The Pressures of Being a Pastor's Wife

In addition to those arising as a result of the problems of the youngsters, there are those directly relating to the wife. I know, in my case, that I can be grateful for a church whose members *individually* don't expect a great deal of me. But *collectively* it all demands much of my time, often more time than I really have. When their children marry or family members die or become injured or ill, even if this doesn't happen more than once or twice a year, in each instance it takes time. Also remember that we have more than 10,000 members at First Baptist in Van Nuys!

Life for Children of Missionaries

Life's pressures are worse, I think, for missionary children. I personally went to school with a number of these kids and saw what the difficulties are. One of the worst is frequent separation from their parents—living not only in the midst of total strangers but, also, totally strange cultures. The disease, the sewerage problems, the lack of good water, these and others proliferate.

But, you know, over the past few years, an interesting and disturbing trend has been emerging. Missionaries and their families, in many instances, return to the United States, are exposed to the wicked, wicked things that are happening here, and end up saying that they'd rather be back on the mission field.

On the good side, missionary kids tend to be independent and self-sustaining. They are usually great self-starters. This is, of course, a result of all the things they've undergone.

The Woman as Family Spokesman

I think women should be able to speak, but I don't think they should overshadow their husbands in this regard. In Anita Bryant's case, this was, I gather, forced upon her. I don't think it was anything she wanted. But I have known families where the men were happy for their wives to be the spokesman. They simply did not wish to have that role.

But, on the other hand, you do have the Biblical admonition in such matters. I've always thought that when you get to a point where there is friction in terms of trying to decide who should do what, God's Word should invariably be the barometer. For one reason or another, there has been an eroding of that foundation, that guide—the Bible as the source of knowledge and advice in our lives. We tend to base so much on emotion, how we feel, and that's terribly dangerous.

I am convinced that a family where the wife takes a kind of leading role is going to suffer. It creates a bad effect upon the children involved who would normally look to the father for guidance. It would be wise for the fathers of this country to take their rightful place, as God intended, and hold onto it. Too many are abdicating this.

Why is that so? I think the media are selling this country a bill of goods, and I think Satan is behind it all. Mind you, I think Satan has always been at work, but this generation is certainly allowing him to have a lot more sway in their lives than previous ones.

Do Many Ministers' Sons Enter the Ministry?

A few years ago, I read that there was an unusual number of ministers' sons in Who's Who in America. I found that very interesting. I can think of Jack MacArthur and then John as local examples. But I also feel that the percentage really isn't very high. The pressures are too great.

Our son Patrick is an example. I know that he was asked from the time he was six or seven years old if he was going to be a minister. It was almost expected of him. He seemed to feel that he had no other choice, and he felt he was constantly being pushed toward the ministry. But he tried to be polite and say he didn't know yet, and smiled, and was nice to everyone, especially the ladies.

Maybe this pressure was the cause of some of his rebellion. Instead of being a minister, he's an actor now. He just happened to be in a high-school play and enjoyed it. He found an outlet for self-expression that he'd never known before.

But I know it'll all work out. Jess and I have given Patrick a Christ-centered upbringing. I am sure whatever direction he's headed in is, to a real degree, temporary, and that the Holy Spirit will bring him back eventually.

Gloria Gaither

How do parents, even Christian parents, let their children down the most?

Losing track of their priorities is certainly one area. Doing good things, even Christian things, that are competitive to being a good parent is not honoring to the Lord in the long run. Children deserve a loving home. There are a million voices calling for our attention, most of which are very good, legitimate things, but we must learn to say "no" to most of them if our stable home is jeopardized. I feel that God's mission in life for any mother is to build a successful home environment; failing this we are failing God.

Aren't we saying, then, that family comes before actual service to the Lord? Therefore, if one wants to be really effective in His service, one shouldn't have a family?

No, I'm not saying that. It certainly hasn't been true in my experience. I think two committed persons can do four times as much; I think having a family only multiplies our effectiveness. It reduces our frustrations as far as feeling secure and loved and important. If that one primary relationship is intact and sure, then it puts you at ease in a thousand other areas that you might question about yourself. If a woman really feels loved by her husband, and valued, then that makes her a better witness for Christ.

A woman's service for Christ can be invalidated only by herself. T. S. Eliot once wrote, "Corruption is never compulsory." No one outside yourself ever corrupts you. Nobody corrupts me. If I yield to the negative influences in my life, I, myself, must take the responsibility. I can't blame my husband and say he isn't a good Christian; I can't blame my situation; or anything else.

How do you think kids let down their parents the most?

Well, I think the original sin of which we all are guilty in that respect is ingratitude. It's the sin that caused Adam and Eve to fall. It was probably the cardinal sin I manifested as a child in regard to my own parents. I'm still probably unaware of the extent of their commitment and sacrifice. Not that we should go around, saying, "I so appreciate your sacrifice." I don't think any parent wants that. I only want my children to take up the stroke for themselves. It's like holding up a swimmer until he gets the hang of it. Then if he can become a strong, self-sufficient swimmer, that's the gratitude we all want shown.

So many parents are afraid of losing their children. What do you think about this?

The whole purpose of being parents is to work ourselves out of a job, really. We're not to raise emotional cripples. We're to raise independent people. They must be capable of standing on their own. Parents who have selfish designs for their children are surely displeasing to the Lord. I see success in *my* job when my daughter Suzanne thinks for herself and makes beautiful, wise decisions without me. She's fourteen years old now. It is such a moving experience for me to be able to see her begin to be a functioning, committed person without using her relationship with me as a crutch.

But I can understand it when parents are reluctant to let go. I think there's something in everybody that wants to hang on. To paraphrase Scripture for a moment, "She who would save her children should be willing to lose them for Christ's sake."

How does the church let down parents and children the most?

Programming them to death. I really have a burden about this. I see church families pulled apart by guilt feelings that the church causes by saying, "You should be here every night for a revival. You should be here every Wednesday night. You should be here every Sunday night. You should be here for every dinner we have. You should be here for Tuesday night Men's Fellowship. You should be here for Women's Missionary Society." The church makes families feel they are second-rate Christians if they aren't participating in all of these activities and fellowships. Yet every night away from home robs something from the family.

I think one of the best, most creative, most honest things the church can do is say, "Let's all commit to spend three nights a week in our own homes, conversing, helping with homework, sharing our day with each other. How can we as a church help you to do that?"

Why is it that the Mormons have such a high success ratio with their family units? More so, in many instances, than fundamental Christians?

The Mormons put the right kind of pressure on families to be together—for fathers and mothers to be present, to be involved with their children. They discourage television or anything else that would take away communication among family members.

Getting back to the role of parents, what about the man in his early twenties who is insecure, neurotic, and filled with anxiety? People tell him, "You can't blame your parents. You can take your life and change it yourself." Is it that easy if his parents have messed up the child so much?

I think when you're old enough to analyze what's going on, and blame your parents, you're old enough to take some of the responsibility. You're old enough to do something about your life, and about your parents' lives, to try putting some good times in theirs. Even if they have failed miserably. If I have enough sense to know that, if I have enough sense to realize what my parents did to me, the damage they inflicted, then as a committed Christian it is my responsibility to ask God to help me begin to forgive and repair my own emotions. And then ask, "How can I change what's left of their lives? How can I as their child put positive things into the time they have before they go into eternity?"

43

Do you find that, as a creative person, you are a better parent, that your creativity is of significant value?

I hope so. For one thing I think it makes me notice and encourage creativity in my children. When I was teaching, I knew so many children whose parents recognized as good in them only those things that would eventually produce income. This was in secular schools. I'm not necessarily talking about the Christian world. Even so parents tend to say, "My son is so talented he could get a really good job and earn a lot of money as a result." Materialism appears in many guises.

One problem, however, Bill and I have run into is that by encouraging creativity so much, we've perhaps allowed a little too much lack of inhibition on their part. If you were to come to my house, for example, my children would approach you and say, "Would you like to hear me play my drums? Would you like to hear the latest poem I wrote?" That sort of thing.

It's good and it's bad. We have to rein them in now and then, telling them not to impose upon people that way unless it's something people really want to know about. "We want you to write your songs, compose your poetry, but be considerate of others," we have to remind them.

But it's good because they certainly are outgoing. They are very good at getting into conversations even in the midst of a brand-new situation involving total strangers. I want them to be aware that every person who walks into our home has something in his life that's just as exciting to him as their poetry or music is to them. If we can learn from the people who enter our home, our lives are enriched as a result.

We try not to allow our children to smart off and talk back to us and be smart-alecky. We want them to be respectful. Still we like to give them opportunity every once in a while to know that whatever they say is going to be accepted, and they don't have to be guarded. So they might say, "Last week when you disciplined me for such and such, you were wrong. You didn't hear me out. I got a spanking for something I should not have been disciplined for because you were in a hurry. You were harried that day; it was a bad one. So your bad day caused my disciplining. And I think that's unfair."

A lot of times they are right. A lot of times I find it necessary, when I have tucked my kids into bed, to say to them, "I didn't do a very good job today of parenting you. What you didn't realize was that before you came home from school a lot happened in my life that made me uptight. I can't help that and neither can you. But what I could have done was not take it out on you, and I'm sorry I did. I've never been a mother before *being* a mother to you. Today I didn't do so well. Let's pray together. And you pray for me; I don't want to repeat myself tomorrow."

Children are marvelously forgiving. I can see this quality time after time. For example: "My teacher needs our prayers. She is having a rough time. I don't know what it is in her life; but for the last week or so she's really been uptight. I know there must be something. I want to be part of the answer."

I think it's vital for families to spend hours together, as I said earlier, to actually know the chemistry of what each other is thinking and feeling. When a child comes home discouraged the parents know right away that this is the case. Because they know that child so well, they can say right away, "What's wrong?"

What happens these days is sad, for so many children have problems that their parents don't sense. Nobody knows them well enough to say, "Something's different about you. The chemistry's wrong. What is it?" I believe we have to spend many, many hours together to know this. My kids will ask of me, "What happened to you, Mom? What's wrong? Can we help?"

Children also need to learn the value of solitude. From morning till night their lives are bombarded with stimulation, with sounds. I believe one gift we can give our children is the gift of silence. I think that kids should know the satisfaction of being alone. This doesn't mean loneliness, but solitude is vital from time to time. Spending moments with nothing happening is delightful. I will not turn on the radio when there's no purpose for doing so. We need to pledge to ourselves: "I will not turn on the television indiscriminately. I will learn to 'hear' solitude and not be uncomfortable." We don't hear much silence these days, you know.

I feel uncomfortable about all the sounds that constantly fill our world. My children have been living in a world where there is no silence as a rule. To find silence we go to the woods and just sit. I let the kids just go and they'll end up sitting by a creek perhaps. I try to teach them to hear the silence, to hear the brook, and to hear a cardinal. I sometimes say, "Do you hear oak leaves? Dead oak leaves sound like leather. There's no other leaf that sounds like an oak leaf when the wind blows it." My children have been taught to hear these things, because, you see, our world spends so much time teaching them to listen to artificial sounds, sounds that wouldn't be there if not created artificially by men.

All of us have to tune these intrusions out or we'll go crazy. The psyche can only handle so much stimulation without cracking up.

What's the greatest frustration you find in being a mother?

I always feel like there's just not enough of me to go around. I'm not wise enough, and I know this. That's why it's important to have the kind of rapport established with my child so that I can go to him or her and say, "I am not God. I was wrong. Let's start over again."

It worries me, this lack of time and attention I just mentioned. I always feel that somebody needed more attention than they got today. But the thing that keeps the joy in being a parent is the fact that I, too, am a becomer. I, too, am a "kid under construction," and my children understand this. So, together, we're growing. Some days I feel like leaving the dishes and the beds unmade, just like the children do, and rolling down the hillside and picking daffodils, which I do. I mean, I do it! And I say to my children, "You're right! This is, right now, the very best use of our time. Not always clearing the table."

A beautiful example of this happened not too long ago. I *was* clearing the table. It was dusk. That day was one of a million things going on. Everybody was harried; Bill was going a thousand different ways. After supper the kids ran outside. It was a balmy evening. We had eaten supper very late, and I was trying to get things cleared so that I could hear their prayers and talk with them. Here again I was trying to do a good thing. I was trying to be a steward of my time in the kitchen so I could have some time later with the kids.

In came Benji and said, "Come here, Mom!"

"I can't," I told him.

"You've got to!" he insisted.

I said, " I can't, Benji. I've got to finish with these dishes. It's already eight o'clock. I can't come. You'll just have to wait."

He told me, "OK, but you're gonna miss it." And he just turned his back and walked out the door.

It dawned on me that this moment was important to him, so I went out the door. The sky was a riot of crimson. It was a beautiful sunset, and across the sky there was a jet line that had come right from the horizon clear up to the top of the sky. It was breathtaking, this white stream against a fiery sky!

We live by a creek and the geese were restless. With the bright sun reflecting on the water, they suddenly took off and went flying across the crimson sky.

Benji reached out and took my hand, totally forgiving what I had said before. "Oh, Mother, I'm so glad you came. Look, there's a ladder clear to Heaven!" And to think that I was so busy that I nearly missed that moment.

So my son and I walked down the hillside and along the creek. We spent another hour just taking everything in. It was a gift from the Lord, those moments, that Benji and I shared.

Anita Bryant

Wherever Anita Bryant goes, they seem to find her. Sometimes there are just a couple of them, sometimes a score or more, these pathetic children of the night. Their faces are occasionally painted in a grotesque imitation of the feminine, moonlight exaggerating the way they look.

Some will laugh but others will wait almost in the shadows, haunted expressions highlighting the sorrow that seems to come from their very spirits. There is certainly no peace even with the ones who make a pretense of being happy. It is a charade, an attempt to present a contented, nonchalant demeanor to the ever-present media.

"Do we look like the condemned?" one gay man will say as he embraces his lover. "We're happy, man. Tell that broad inside we're happy."

Not so.

Gays are living under a delusion that their peers are so afraid of acknowledging that they must reinforce it in a variety of ways

Ruth Graham

Laura Lee Oldham

Julia Staton

Macel Falwell

Joyce Fasi

Virginia Womach

Evelyn Christenson

Betty Criswell

Gloria Hope Hawley

Patti Lewis

Nancy Schumacher

Evelyn LeTourneau

or else lose their very sanity. They'd laugh at you if you proposed this to them, but there can be no other explanation for the obsessive need they have to go to gay barbers, lawyers, dentists, and so on. They crave the affirmation of other gay people. It is a narcotic without which they would be faced with the reality, the truth of their condition.

Understanding the depth of sickness, of sin to which the homosexual is prone, heightens the justice of Anita Bryant's campaign. If you have ever counseled with an emotional teenager caught up in the gay world, particularly that part of it which demands that they sell their bodies to anyone willing to pay the price, if you have ever heard them cry their hearts out and beg for release, then you realize that all of the liberal nonsense that would permit free exercise of homosexual "rights" is but nihilistic, satanic propaganda of the most corrupting sort. Even the non-Christian organization, American Psychiatric Association, can no longer be considered an ally of the gay cause. In 1978 the APA reversed itself and labeled "gayness" a sickness.

Anita knows all of this. That is why she and husband Bob Green have been starting gay counseling centers across the United States.

"We have reached nearly 3000 young people for Christ," she told me with justifiable pride, "and they have given up the gay life altogether as a result."

A woman who hates homosexuals, as gay activists would like everyone to believe is the case, would not be going to the time, trouble, and expense of commencing these centers.

Enough of the specifically gay question for a moment. We'll get back to it, briefly, in a bit. For, you see, one of the side effects of Anita's speaking out is that attention has been focused on the more sensational ramifications, but much less has been detailed as to why. And that is foundational to every purpose of this book. It is part of the motivation of every mother interviewed—the stability of the home.

"We need to put on the whole armor of God," she said. "The spiritual warfare into which we are being thrust is being waged by the Enemy at many levels, but none that is more devastating, potentially, than his attacks on the family unit.

"Sin can start like a cancer. But the denial syndrome kicks in and we find ourselves denying that there is any problem. In the old days sin was thought of as a little like leprosy. When the first sore appeared, nobody thought anything of it. Maybe it was even ignored. When it became larger some medicine was put on it, and maybe it was patched up. Yet, eventually, it spread up the arm and then over the whole body. We should revive that description today.

"The breakdown in a family can start in a seemingly insignificant way. Then all of a sudden something else happens and the family deteriorates. Even Christians are doing or permitting things these days that would never have been allowed a few years ago. Certain movies are accepted. Then there is smoking, drinking. All these and more are eating away at the Christian home and individual lives.

"We cannot compromise with sin. But this is happening in the church as well as the home. It's not just the homosexuals who are compromising. Not just the feminists. Not just the people who think they have a right to kill babies. Or the kids who want to go on drugs for escape and eventually blow out their minds. It's all of these and more, in and out of the Christian world.

"Maybe we have really preached too cheap a grace. If it's easy to get into, it's easy to disregard, to throw back in God's face."

Anita then brought up a point that many pastors will not want to hear about. It strikes at the heart of those who would brag about how much money they've collected on a given Sunday, or how many new members or how great a new building—crystal or otherwise—is going to be built.

"We've become so concerned with the material things, the numbers, the edifices," she said, "that we seem to have forgotten that the new members inside these grand and glorious buildings need counseling. We act as though once a member becomes a statistic on an attendance chart that is that, and interest in that member drops."

"All right, Anita," I asked, "how would you go about witnessing to a mother who comes to you and says, 'Look, I'm not a Christian. Yet I believe as you do about the homosexual issue. I believe in a close family and all of the other moral values you talk about. But I'm not a Christian. Why should I bother to become one?' How would you convince her? She's everything you are from a moral and ethical point of view—and probably an extremely good mother. Everything, that is, except Christ is not her Savior and Lord. What difference, can you tell her, *would* Christ make in the family life she enjoys now?"

"First, let me say that many, many of the people who agree with me on the moral issues do not agree on the spiritual ones. I have no problems in terms of working with them. We have joined together for a mutually worthwhile purpose.

"Hopefully the best approach is by my example. If an individual saw through my consistency something special in my life, like the mother you mentioned, and was curious as to why I am a Christian if, outwardly, there is little difference in our lifestyles, I would have to be perfectly honest and just take her back to the Bible. I would say that our life here on earth is very short when you compare it to eternity, and that either Christ is what He said He is, or He's the greatest liar ever to deceive human beings.

"We are not just a physical body. We are not just a soul that has a will, an intellect, emotions. The Bible says we are a spiritual being. What happens here determines the ultimate destiny of that spiritual part of man.

"I would try to point out to such a mother that the Bible is God's inspired Word, and to share with her who He is, His person, His character, His authority, and all the rest. But it is necessary that such a woman have at least a modicum of belief in Someone up there. If she doesn't, it's next to impossible to reach her during one conversation or even a dozen. The Lord would have to step in mightily in that case.

"But if there were the slightest opening, then I'm sure the Holy Spirit would provide the words that would pierce her heart."

. . . that would pierce her heart.

As Anita spoke great concern was reflected in her eyes. We were sitting in the Protect America's Children office in Miami Beach. On the walls were awards she had won, photos of herself, Bob Green, others. Several family shots were there.

Anyone spending an "honest" few minutes with her, with an open mind that wasn't boiling over with preconceptions, would see how sensitive she is, how concerned over the salvation of souls. I remember some time we spent together in El Paso in 1978. She was introduced to an ex-member of the gay community who was, at the least, skeptical about her intentions, her motivations. He went away from Anita, after an hour or so with her, willing to evaluate his ideas about her.

"And, you know," Anita continued, "I would try to show such a mother that there is nothing she can present to the Lord as far as good works, morality, anything other than Christ, that will suffice in the presence of a Holy God. I would tell her of many instances of lives changed as a result of redemption. We can grab after everything but the Lord and, in the long run, find our lives to be little more than empty farces. When someone is facing death without Christ, the fear, the regret, the terror must be overwhelming."

Indeed it must. I know someone, a longtime friend of the family, who has traveled extensively, who can buy anything he wants anytime he wants it, but who has regularly rejected the validity, the necessity of having Christ in his life. He thinks he is happy. He has the physical manifestations of material security all around him. He knows many people. He has a well-organized life-style. He is content.

For now.

But what about later? He has only a few years left until his ninetieth birthday. It could happen anytime. He has no family—he never married, in fact. Friends have a habit of disappearing, so it is not impossible that there will be no one around when he dies, except hired doctors and nurses monitoring his heart, his lungs, his brain waves. Death will come when that heart ceases beating, those lungs breathe in no more air, and the brain goes blank.

Gone.

What has it all meant—the travel; the cars; the houses; the money; the friends? No children to stand by him; no one left, for he's outlived them all.

"With Jesus Christ there is everything," Anita said softly. "There's a peace that truly passes all understanding. I've met so many people who have everything the world can offer. They've tried to sustain happiness, but in the end it all crumbles, passing like sand between their fingers. Nothing can compare with the kind of assurance that comes when the Holy Spirit takes up residence within us."

But so often we let the Lord down in so many ways. He has given us everything, and yet we often end up each day having returned nothing. We must cause Him a special kind of disillusionment when this occurs. Knowing this, His promise of never leaving, never forsaking us is all the more wonderful.

"I read in one of your books, Anita, that you admitted to having a temper. Is that still the case? Or have you more or less conquered it?" I asked.

"I have to admit to still displaying it from time to time. I think maybe the Lord's gotten a little further in His goal of having me quiet that temper altogether—but my husband's not so sure at times.

"Let me make a point here: All my life God's *had* to show me that, without Him, I am nothing. Sure, there's been improvement—but I often think that we never totally eliminate these thorns in the flesh. If we did, we might think that we no longer need His control, that we can handle any situation ourselves.

"No, I have to confess daily some weakness, some sin to Him. Confessing and repenting is an in-one-sitting act of getting really right with the Lord. I have to put myself on that cross, in a sense.

"As a mother I see, constantly, that it's the little things, the moments that seem so unimportant, that can rise up to haunt us in our relationships with our children."

Anita was obviously very concerned about how she conducted herself in front of her family. She felt an adoration for her children that was clear as she talked, especially about the encroachments of the gay movement on young people in general.

"All of a sudden we have homosexuals as so-called positive role models, whereas half a century ago they were abhorred," she said. "A young man, wavering in his sexual identity, is able to find social images that are appealing rather than disgusting."

The novelist who freely admits his homosexuality; the lesbian "couple" pulling at the heartstrings as they beg for understanding, for compassion in their effort to adopt a child; the situation comedies that treat homosexuality in a light vein, with no condemnation whatsoever, these are the models that such a young man has today. Children under attack—a real danger, a satanic plot that spreads ever more deeply into the mainstream of life.

But not all dangers come from the gay movement. Some stem from parents themselves.

"We tend to worship our ministers, our leaders, our artists, our writers even," I pointed out. "And some parents tend to—"

"—worship their children," Anita finished the sentence for me. "I'm vulnerable in that respect. I think we all want to be able to trust other individuals, to look at them with respect and, sometimes, awe. Mothers become convinced that their youngsters can do no wrong, no *serious* wrong, in any event. They spoil their sons, their daughters. So many children seem able to snap their fingers and their parents will jump and do anything they want."

Such a parental approach leads to adults who are "screaming women demanding everything under the sun," as Anita put it.

"What bothers me terribly," she continued, "is not so much the women themselves as rather the impact upon the children they have brought into the world. Hosea 4:6 is especially revealing: 'My people are destroyed for lack of knowledge . . . seeing thou has forgotten the law of thy God, I will also forget thy children.'

"Isn't that frightening? The same group in favor of abortion shows the same murderous perspective *vis-a-vis* ERA. They seem not to care about the next generation which they are supposed to be shepherding. Kill them before they're born or mess up the minds, the emotions of those who *are* born. It's all the same to these women. What they exhort the rest of us to is a kind of ultimate selfishness, the end product of caring about themselves even if it means destroying innocent, often totally helpless lives."

. . . *innocent* . . . *helpless.*

Oh, yes. Especially the runaways. The million kids annually. Wandering the streets. Doing anything, *anything* for a few bucks. Some, astonishingly, come from Christian homes. Some claim to have "accepted Christ into their lives" a long time ago.

And what about the runaway *parents?* You don't hear as much about them. The kids get the headlines. But there are many thousands of mothers and fathers who abandon their families. That leads to even more damaged young lives. Maybe these kids will never run away as their fathers or their mothers have or as so many of their peers do but, emotionally, psychologically, the havoc is going to be incalculable.

Christians *must not* expect family life to be free of pain, of anguish, even if no member runs away or gets hung up on drugs or engages in an illicit sexual relationship.

Anita has not had to face anything like what was just mentioned, but she has had anxious moments. No, that's too superficial a way of expressing what she's gone through over the years. Let Anita's description of something fairly recent suffice:

"I took our daughter Barbara up to the Mayo Clinic. God really answered prayers, Roger. We fasted and prayed for quite a while about her. The doctors had narrowed it down to either a particular growth that would have to be removed from her hip or else rheumatoid arthritis. I wanted another set of opinions and that's why we went to Mayo."

While she and Bob and Barbara were there, they spent some time with Edith and Francis Schaeffer. Anita felt her own trust in God strengthened as a result of observing this remarkable couple.

Then, weeks later, after the prayers, the fasting, they learned that little Barbara's condition was not serious; indeed, it would in time clear up completely.

"Then Bob's mother, my mother-in-law, went into the hospital supposedly for a tumor on one of her ovaries. Well, we committed her to everyone in a special prayer chain—and, yes, the tumor ended up being dissolved without an operation."

Being a Christian means not *escaping* these moments of crisis but, rather, finding the strength to endure them.

"Anita," I said near the conclusion of our interview, "what is the ultimate security available to every Christian mother?"

"God's promises are many," she replied. "But there are three that, in my opinion, remain at the forefront when it comes to a mother looking at her children, reflecting upon the years of love and work that she has lavished upon them, and wondering in her heart just what the future holds."

At home she can control the circumstances, to a degree. At home she can offer an environment that filters out a host of the negativisms that proliferate in the "outside" world. But one day all this will change. One day—.

"The first is, 'Greater is He who is in you than he who is in the world.' We could add, legitimately, 'Greater is he that is in you *and your children.*' The second is this: 'If God is for us, who is against us?' But the third is really the capstone: 'No man is able to pluck them out of my Father's hand.' "

They'll come back eventually if they are born again in the first place. And no one—not the pimps, the men who rent their bodies, the pushers, no one—can change any process which the Lord oversees.

"Not in the long run," Anita added. "No more than was the case with the prodigal son. What a comfort! The greatest comfort any mother can experience even when it seems her heart will break into a hundred irreparable pieces."

Carole Carlson

Like Carole Carson, the rest of us expect death. It is part of the price paid for Eden and the fall. When someone reaches the age of seventy, we start talking of "the years left." For some it may not be even one year but, rather, months or, perhaps, weeks.

There are those who don't reach their seventies. They die at sixty-five. Or fifty-five. Or forty.

Or—

The younger the person, the more tragic death seems, at least in earthly terms. We weep over opportunities stilled for all time. We think of joy here, in the flesh, that will never be experienced. With so much talk about the average life expectancy increasing, the shock of someone dying before a certain age hits home.

Gone—as a vapor, a phantom, or so it could appear to those of us struggling with our memories, our minds playing such tricks on us as to make us conjecture, in a moment of sorrow, "I knew him. I loved him. But he was taken so quickly. I wonder, I wonder if—he—ever—existed."

The mind, in sudden moments of sorrow fed by loneliness and remembered vignettes from the past, plays tricks, deceives us, and then reality returns. We get up and go on, somehow, putting our scrapbooks and necklaces and shoes worn by the deceased many years ago into a drawer or cedar chest. Not thinking of them, really thinking of them again, for maybe a year or several years. But we always *do* return, because when we *care*, when we care *that* much, return is inevitable.

Carole Carlson had son Kent taken from her when there was no way to have expected the event. He was to have come back from his plane trip and rejoined the family circle as always. Countless times he had piloted that plane. Countless times he had said, *"Good-bye, Mother, I love you, I'll be back soon."* He would have shaken his father Ward's hand and spoken of his love for this man who was at the same time his dearest, closest pal. And he would be gone.

Then he *was* gone. With a sudden, awful, eerie finality. . . .

"You have experienced a tragedy that many people, indeed most, never undergo," I said as Carole and I sat in the living room of the home that had been hers and Ward's and Kent's and the two other children's for nearly two decades.

A word about this home. You step into it and love dances about the corridors. You can feel love within its confines. You sense with total conviction that those living in there, past and present, were/are knit together by the sweetest, most enduring love of which sinful man is capable. Love for each other, love for their Savior and Lord.

"Is there anything," I continued, "that you've especially learned from this experience? So many people I know are nominal Christians who make a habit of professing their faith when things are going along well. But when tragedy strikes they start to go to pieces, questioning the Lord, agonizing about why He would allow such and such to happen. You and Ward are different. What held the two of you together?"

"I think that what impressed me *after* the shock and the pain subsided was the importance of having your children know the Lord when they are small. Without the knowledge that your child is walking the streets of Heaven, well, the experience can be absolutely devastating. The Lord doesn't bring such things into our lives to punish us but to make us grow, to mature in Him."

It was in his blood, just like his dad's, Carole wrote. *When they flew together, or talked about flying, they were in another world. It was a world of freedom, of pitting their skill against the vastness of the sky . . . a world where beauty could be described by the expression on his face.*

"We came to realize," Carole continued, "that we were given the privilege to have a child for a certain length of time, and he was not ours to own, but ours to cherish and love for the years he was with us. After he was taken away, there were things we needed to say to other parents as far as their relationships with their children were concerned.

"Knowing what can happen makes your time with your child so much more precious. You should love that child almost as though tomorrow will be his last day on this earth. That doesn't mean to smother him. But it does mean not to take him for granted. It's almost like preventive medicine. The people who show that they can't cope with tragedy are the ones who have been, in no way, prepared for it."

"Have you come across people—"

My thoughts drifted for a second as I was asking this next question. Pictures of Kent were on the wall. He was a fine looking, blonde-haired young man. His personality must have been something, as the expression goes. I thought, foolishly, how hard I took it when a pet of mine died, how I mourned for days. But just an animal! Here a *human* life was no more. . . .

"—who have said to you that they have had so much tragedy with their children that they think, sometimes, it might have been better never to have had children than to have lost them so soon?"

"Oh, yes. Not long after Kent was killed—"

So easy to say it. No tears come, at least outwardly. It has been said before—many times. Kent is dead. Years after the crash, years after that awful day, it is possible to say *Kent is dead* and not collapse into a sobbing bundle of self-pity.

"—a neighbor's daughter of the same age as Kent was killed in a car accident. Immediately when we learned of this, Ward and I walked into that home. They just looked at us and said, 'We thought you'd come.' Their reaction was, 'Why should we have children when it is necessary to cope with this sort of thing?'

"Yet it's a relationship that's so precious. We have to realize that we raise our children to a certain age and do the best we possibly can, and then they leave. Some leave forever, as far as this life is concerned anyway. Some leave to build lives of their own. Either way, we must learn to let go. We can't punish our-selves with guilt or sorrow or whatever. That's not the answer."

"Oppressive sorrow can be Satan's weapon," I added. "Some parents go so far as to set aside a room of belongings and such, and never really disturb that room again, keeping it as a kind of memorial. It's almost as though they expect to go in one day and find the nightmare over and their child sleeping or studying."

"I have known people like that, yes," Carole said. "In fact, once, when we went to Israel, this couple immediately gravitated to us because of a common tragedy. They told us about having this shrine, so to speak, that they had made of their boy's room. I looked the mother in the eye and said, 'That's a terrible mistake. That's an awful mistake. When they're gone, they're gone. You keep the memory intact, of course, but not the tangible things. That only makes it hurt all the longer.' "

She paused, her eyes a little misty perhaps, then went on. "It's only a matter of self-pity, especially if you're a Christian parent. All of us 'enjoy' indulging ourselves in self pity from time to time. I remember Ward encountering me one day, three or four weeks after Kent's death. I was in the kitchen, breaking down at the sink, sobbing to myself and—"

Up, up the long delirious burning blue I've topped the windswept heights with easy grace, where never lark or even eagle flew; with silent lifting mind I've trod the high untrespassed sanctity of space, put out my hand, and touched the face of God. . . .

"—Ward came up to me and shook me and said, 'Kent is gone, Carole. The sooner you realize that and accept it as real, the better you are going to be.' He was very strong and very firm with me. He loves me very much. He loved Kent very much. It was the best thing he ever did for me. I find it difficult but kind to do that with other people."

"Did you have to help Ward in any way? You just told of an instance where he helped you. Were you able to reciprocate?"

"Oh, I know we helped each other tremendously. A man is programmed in terms of being manly and controlling his emo-tions. I don't think I'd ever seen Ward break down and be so very emotional. The tenderness of our relationship grew wonderfully during that time. It brought us so much closer together. It can work that way or in the opposite direction."

"Closer together or further apart?" I asked.

"Right. In my case I needed to be a source of strength for him, too. He had a son who was his pal. They flew together. They used to get up at 5:00 in the morning and—"

Hurry, Dad.

Okay, Son.

Beautiful day.

You're so right, Kent.

Thank you, Dad.

For what, Son?

For being the way you are.

"They were flying before Kent ever went to school. They were close, very, very close.

"Despite our loss, despite the tears and all the rest, we knew we couldn't continue with our grief because we had other children who had experienced the loss, too. We couldn't just live on in the sad memories of a situation we wouldn't ever change. I began to see that I was starting to neglect our younger son. He was living in the shadow of the memory of his older brother. He was beginning to think he was a second-class citizen."

"This is a dangerous matter. I have seen it happen in other families. The grief is so profound that the living are neglected."

Carole added, "The greatest concern I have today is over the disintegration of the Christian family. Particularly at the level of those who have been in positions of influence in the Christian community."

"To what do you attribute this?"

"Ironically, their effectiveness for Christ. They have been effective for the work of the Lord, and anyone who is effective that way is going to be the target of the enemy, Satan.

"Where is Satan going to place his barbs? At the point of most severe weakness. If a man or woman, who has been in the Lord's service, has put the Lord first to the point where other aspects of his life are definitely secondary, then that is where Satan will attack. Of course, as they have problems with their families, those outside of the Christian community look at them and think if that's what a Christian family is supposed to be, forget it."

"We elevate people to positions of super spirituality, and there is no such thing as a super spiritual person," I added.

"They are idolized and almost worshiped. Put right on their little pedestals. That is a great tragedy, Roger. There is no other subject, no other concern on the American Christian scene that is more crucial than the strengthening of the family. Unless we are more perceptive within the Christian community as to family needs and our support of each other, we're going to find, first of all, that our families will fall apart. From that point our witness to the world will crumble, and, after that, our country goes the same route."

I had no feeling. I knew where Kent was at that very moment and I was in awe, realizing that my crazy blonde streak, a part of my body and the son of the man I loved, was with the God of the universe.

Carole and Ward and the other children had strength to face not only the normal, everyday demands of familyhood but even the extraordinary, the unexpected.

As she wrote, in *Straw Houses in the Wind*, "While governments are staggering, and people are viewing every shadow on the street with suspicion, what a need there is to encourage one another! Never before has it been so important as it is right now, in what many of us believe is the countdown on God's timetable for history, to draw together in the love of Christ, to exhibit the fruit of the love triangle, and to provide that encouragement."

. . . encouragement.

When Carole needed this most, encouragement was given. By family. By friends. By the Holy Spirit himself. They had lost so much. Ever so often a memory will, even today, filter up from her subconscious and she will relive something.

"We used to play this little game of musical beds," Carole said, smiling at the recollection. "I know what psychiatrists say about the danger of homosexuality if this happens with the boys in any family. But that's nonsense, in my opinion. They crawl into bed with Mommy and Daddy for security. What's wrong with that? This child psychology gobbledygook is given more credence than it deserves.

"There was the time Kent watched me throw a temper tantrum—literally throw a temper tantrum. I was so furious with him for something. He stood, and looked at me, and said, 'Mother, I can't believe that it's you.' I stopped right there, hesitated, then started to laugh because I heard my own words coming right back at me."

She continued, "We always did things together as a family. We took trips together. We've tried to expose our children to travel, especially in the United States. I love teaching children to be proud of being Americans, to love our country, to respect our flag. We always fly the flag on all holidays. When our children got into the era, in the 1960's, when it was unpopular to respect the flag, when it wasn't 'cool' to be a red-blooded American, Karen especially went along with her peers for awhile. But it was always back to what Mom and Dad taught.

"It's fun to be a mother. It's fun to do things with your kids. You should start as many activities as you can, for the time you have together is precious. You'll never know when a relationship with a son might be terminated. Take the moments you have. Cherish them. There is a lot of talk among women about youthfulness, you know, good skin care and health and such. I would say to another woman, 'The best way to stay young is to have children. And the best way to stay younger is to hope you have grandchildren.' "

Joann Letherer

I had known Von Letherer for a couple of years before I started reading Joyce Landorf's book, *Mourning Song*. It was apparent that he had some difficulty walking. I thought perhaps that it was due to an injury or some other "obvious" cause.

Then I came upon Joyce's dedication page:

> This book is lovingly dedicated to
> Von Letherer

> A man who has courageously faced and coped with death and dying for all of his thirty-seven years. His life as a dauntless Christian and his remarkable silence through the years of his pain-filled illness have honed and refined him into a dangerously beautiful, Christlike man.
> The song of mourning constantly swirls about him, yet the clear, ringing, dolce melody of Christ's love is never lost or obscured.

In hearing the spirited bravura of this man's music, our hearts have been lifted toward Christ and we have been deeply touched—we will never be the same again!

I was stunned. What could Joyce be referring to in her dedication? When I phoned her, she said, simply, "Talk to Von. It's a story you'll never forget."

I did just that, and suggested that an interview with Joann and Von might be a very worthwhile addition to this book, since she has shared his ordeal for the twenty years of their marriage.

But what was that ordeal? What had been at the root of Von's having to cope "with death and dying" for all of his life?

As I drove to Reflections Restaurant in Glendale, I wondered how many people walking the streets of every village, town, and city in the country are experiencing traumas of one sort or another; who might be living with constant pain; who might be on the verge of suicide because life has become too harsh for them. Von, for example, seemed to be smiling a lot as I recalled our meetings in the past. He was far from a somber soul, according to memory. Yet, apparently, his ordeal was far above the ordinary.

For Joann the struggles must have been difficult. To face a marriage relationship with someone you love who is in never-ending discomfort, at the very least, she had to have a very special brand of tenacity.

As I approached the restaurant, I considered all the superficial people who become upset if they have a slight headache. If they have to wait in line three minutes too long at an airport ticket counter, they berate the clerk who is obviously doing his best in a frantic situation. If they find the temperature some days five degrees too warm, they complain of the "beastly" weather and moan and groan as though the world is about to end. If they don't have their martinis on time, if they don't start their cars the first turn of the key, the rest of the day is ruined for them.

How petty! I said to myself. *Life for them is based upon convenience. Take that away even for an instant, and they are pathetically miserable in soul and spirit.*

Joann and Von and I sat in the waiting area of Reflections. Our table—in a "quiet" corner—would be ready shortly. In the meantime we commenced the interview.

Von is a hemophiliac.

As a child and young person growing up, a simple injury

could have been the prelude to his bleeding to death. I remember seeing John Travolta in a TV movie entitled *The Boy in the Glass Bubble*. It was about a young man who had to be kept isolated from the world around him because of the danger of bacterial infection. Von's situation is a far cry from that, but learning of his hemophilia evoked images of that movie. He *does* have to be exceptionally careful. Can you *imagine* going through life with the fear that even a slight bruise could be disastrous? Can you imagine being concerned about nicking yourself on a rough piece of metal? Can you—?

What, briefly, *is* hemophilia?

For one thing it is primarily hereditary; and it occurs usually among men. (There are only a few cases on record of women suffering from it!) But, ironically, it is inherited through the mother, not the father.

A man suffering from hemophilia has a condition characterized by delayed clotting of the blood and a consequent abnormal tendency to bleed or hemorrhage. This is due to plasma deficiency in the bloodstream.

Bleeding can take place without being caused by a cut or laceration. Bleeding can start from emotional stress, or climate changes. Also hemorrhages over the years cause great damage and crippling.

Life with a hemophiliac is not easy for the woman who chooses to marry one. She must, as the expression goes, do so with her eyes wide open.

That Joann did. God prepared her for the task of caring for Von in a very special way. She had no illusions.

They met at a youth camp when she was just twelve years old. He was fifteen at the time. They were very fond of each other right from the beginning.

"I'm going to marry you someday," he told her as they sat together under a huge shade tree.

She smiled because she had been thinking along much the same lines. True they were "only kids," but it seemed that God had drawn them close for a special reason that neither could ascertain. They sensed that being husband and wife was their ordained destiny.

He told her about himself, keeping nothing back.

Fifteen months old. That's when his parents and he had discovered the nature of his condition.

Bruises. All over his body.

These kept increasing in number and severity. Finally they took him to a small town doctor who knew very little about hemophilia. (It should be noted that no one else in the medical profession had much insight in those days about the disease.)

"You must be kind and loving," the doctor told them in his warm, well-meaning way. "Take him home. Be careful with him. Your son is very ill. The first bad fall in which he cuts or bruises himself seriously will cause his death. Love him, hold him, be thankful for him as long as he has left."

He had to restrict himself—no more rough-and-tumble playing. He was doomed to an abbreviated life of isolation.

Despite his parents' best efforts he fell down and cut his lip and began to bleed. They were unable to stop it.

They rushed him back to the country doctor.

"Nothing we can do," the doctor said. "Take him home. Put ice on the wound. Possibly, after a period of time, it will stop, but if it doesn't he will be gone."

Fortunately the Letherers lived near the University of Michigan Hospital in Ann Arbor. So they took Von there where, after admission, he was given a pint of whole blood. The bleeding stopped immediately.

"Why did you allow your son to be nearly dead before you brought him here?" a doctor asked. All they could do was profess ignorance. . . .

This was a little of what Von told Joann that day at camp. He didn't want to deceive her. Having her know the absolute truth was essential. Though he felt he would marry her one day, he made it clear that he perhaps might not live long enough to keep that "promise."

She understood. She grew to love him all the more. Seven years later, with many opportunities to know what life as Von's wife could mean, she married him. They began an exciting and blessed life together as one. God had a very special life planned for them—one with much suffering and pain, but also one with much joy and peace.

Since hemophilia is a hereditary disease, Von and Joann were concerned about having their own children. After inquiring about adoption, they were told by the agency that they wouldn't even do a case study because Von had already lived beyond his life expectancy.

So they prayed for boys, and one happy day Jeff was born.

During the time that they were expecting their second child, Joann became ill. Unable to make a diagnosis, the doctor hospitalized her for further tests. A blood specialist was called in; in fact he was Von's doctor, a hematologist.

"One of the tests made was a bone marrow from my chest. I really sensed that something very serious was wrong. One morning I asked the doctor straight out if I had leukemia. He replied, "No, but you do have Hodgkin's disease."

More common among men than women—though, unlike hemophilia, women do suffer from it. It is not inherited. The cause is unknown.

While resembling cancer, it is also infectious in origin as opposed to being truly malignant. Treatment is of the symptoms rather than the disease, usually with radiation or nitrogen mustard or other drugs. It is always fatal, usually with death coming within a period of two to four years. Even the exceptions live only twenty years more at best.

Joann had it.

"It was a shock and yet it wasn't a shock," she said. "Somewhere in my spirit I had felt that something was very wrong."

Knowing her condition, the doctor asked, "Do you really want this baby?"

"Definitely," she replied. "There's no question about it."

He went on to tell her that because of the nature of the disease, they would have to do X-ray treatment.

"Lymph glands, of course, are all over your body," he added.

That much radiation directed at her when she was pregnant!

"They traced my history back to some problems I had had earlier, physical problems that were never diagnosed. It was a long time ago, too, and the disease had been taking hold ever since. In other words it had progressed far enough that my survival was at stake.

"The night before they were to take me to surgery, a nurse came in and wanted to give me a sleeping pill. But I told her no, that I wanted to fall asleep naturally.

"Through that night I prayed and I read Scripture. The Lord gave me specific verses that were a tremendous encouragement. One of these said, 'In the shadow of thy wings will I make my refuge, until these calamities be overpast.' And I sang quite a bit. I sang, 'In times like these you need a Savior,' and other hymns of comfort. It was a very special time. I asked the Lord to spare my life because our son Jeff was only two and he needed me, as did my husband. I really believed that I was tangible evidence of God's love and care regarding Von. I was convinced that God had chosen me to share Von's life, the pain and the suffering he was always to experience.

"I didn't sleep the entire night. When they came in the next morning to take me to surgery, I was at complete peace, knowing that I was in the Lord's hands. No matter what happened, I knew that He loved me and that He cared for all of us. After the surgery—a test, really, to determine the seriousness of my condition—I was taken back to my room. They sent the gland they had removed to pathology right away, but getting the results took the entire day. My parents were with me, and Von was with me. We waited together. At six o'clock the doctor came and gave us the report."

Nothing! He was astonished.

They had not been able to find *any* trace of cancer. It was a case, as the doctor observed, where "nature had triumphed over science. You would call it a miracle."

Seven months later Greg was born!

Two very special gifts from the Lord—Jeff and Greg. But Von had one more desire—he wished for a little girl. (You know how dads feel about little girls.) Then five years after Greg came, Von and Joann were able to adopt little Julie. What a joy! The Lord's very special gift to fulfill the "desires of their hearts."

So much that fathers and mothers take for granted has been denied Joann and Von. Playing with the kids, for example.

"Roughhousing them is pretty much out," Von commented. "Of course I miss doing this. During the first eight to ten years of their lives I was good enough yet so that, at times, I could get away with tumbling with them. But even then I paid for it. Sure, there was a risk. If you lose, it still was fun, and you gamble on the outcome because of that fun. As I've gotten more and more crippled up and unable to do much, I have had to give up those moments with my children."

"The children have been wonderful," Joann commented. "They will go to any length to make life easier for their dad, and this is always spontaneous with them. They do it out of love and respect. They are very strong in character, very responsible and stable children, especially in their relationship to the Lord.

"Oh, there were occasions when Jeff was very young that he especially felt a great deal of anger. He could not understand why God allowed his father to suffer so much. It didn't make sense to him. In fact, Jeff had such a fear of losing his father that he often denied Von's existence. At school Jeff would never talk about his dad, and so his teacher assumed he didn't have one. The school psychologist spent some time with Jeff, and it was determined that Jeff had seen so much suffering in Von that this was the only way his mind could handle it outside the home.

"Jeff is a very sensitive boy, and he has tremendous devotion to his father. I don't think that you can watch a person constantly go through excruciating pain and not have it rough and gruesome. Jeff saw his dad whisked off to the hospital repeatedly.

"You hurt with that person you love. You enter into that suffering with them. So our children have entered into Von's suffering. Yet we have decided that the blessings so far outweigh anything negative."

Most people don't know what hemophilia is. Of those who do, there are precious few who understand it is far more crippling than arthritis. In fact, it frequently leads to a severe form of arthritis.

"In years past whenever I'd bump my knee, I'd start hemorrhaging profusely in the joint. The average person would be able to go to a doctor, having him aspirate that joint by drawing out the fluid. In my case they didn't dare do that. To stick a needle in my joint would aggravate the problem.

"Thus, every time I had a joint hemorrhage, it was very damaging. The fluid left in there became cartilage, which created very acute arthritis. I am now suffering the consequences."

Nearly all hemophiliacs Von's age—he's in his early forties—are badly crippled. Nowadays younger hemophiliacs can be treated by a new form of concentrate so the damage to their bodies can be minimized. But for Von the damage has already been done.

Painful.

Steady and seldom relieved. Getting up out of a chair. Climbing into or out of a car. Extremely painful.

It would be foolish to say that Von has learned to be grateful for the agony.

"There's no way I can do that," he admitted. "I would be lying. But I have reached a point where I am thankful that I am yet alive and can daily see God's uses for my daily pain."

Joann added, "I think both Von and I have lived with this situation long enough so that we recognize the fact that suffering is a part of our lives in one form or another. Whether it's physical, emotional, whatever, God allows suffering. The fact that we recognize this and accept it as much as we can has enabled us to take it and use it in a positive way, without assuming that it's a punishment."

"Joann is a very unusual person," Von said. "You know, she could just mother me—which would make it worse. It's all right for somebody to sympathize and to be concerned, but nobody likes to have someone else smother and mother them to death. Joann sensed this. There were times when she knew I needed a shoulder to cry on but other times that she said, 'Hey, you're the man of this house. You have to carry a certain amount of responsibility.' So she has, at times, forced me to play the role that I *should* assume. She refused to make it easy for me to feel sorry for myself and moan that I wasn't like other guys."

Every day there is deterioration. He walks a little more slowly. He stands with greater difficulty. There is an increase in the pain. What lies ahead is more of the same, and worse. Someday Von will probably be confined to a wheelchair. Eventually, he may be able to do nothing but sit there, immobile.

"I believe that God has something special for both of us," Joann told me. "But it *is* very hard to deal with, emotionally, when you have to stand by and watch someone you love suffer so much. To think you'll have to live with that for the rest of your married lives."

Only someone like Joann could have dealt with the daily pressure. But even amidst the gratitude she feels at being healed herself, and the preparation she had for the responsibility of being Von's wife, there is a potential source of emotional pain. She was healed but Von hasn't been. Because of this there are always "Job's friends" around who insist that Von has unconfessed sin in his life, that he is out of fellowship with the Lord, and so on.

Yet Joann and Von have turned a potential problem into a victory for Christ.

"People forget so fast," he said. "Joann was healed, and thus that crisis is over. But I'm a daily example. They can't forget what the Lord has done in my life, what He gives me daily in terms of strength, what He does to help this entire family along. Every time they see me, they are reminded."

70

They are prepared for death, this remarkable couple. It doesn't scare them.

"I've gone past the life expectancy that doctors said I would achieve. You know, I've lived a full life. If I were to die tonight, I've still been able to do a lot of living. I have three lovely children, a beautiful wife, and I have no regrets."

Patricia MacArthur

John MacArthur is rapidly becoming known and respected as one of the finest Bible teachers in the country. As pastor of Grace Community Church in Southern California, he has seen the congregation grow from a humble beginning to its present size of more than 5000 members.

Patricia MacArthur is no less conservative than her husband in most matters. Both of them are convinced that the strength of the American family must be maintained without further erosion, that it is being attacked constantly by worldly/satanic intrusions which are increasing in number and momentum. If the family falls, the country will soon follow it, for this has been the way other great civilizations have gone in the past, toppled when the family ceased to be an important factor.

The Three Mistakes Most Parents Make

I think perhaps one of the most prevalent would be the lack of consistency in the application of standards upon their children. They either deviate from these to the extent that the standards become meaningless—or else the parents themselves don't live by the same rules.

I have the impression that, secondly, parents tend to be either too permissive or too legalistic in their approach. Legalism can produce rebellion, whereas standards that are learned and adopted sincerely, as coming from the heart, that is received willingly, tend to stay with a young person through every stage of his life.

A third mistake is pampering young people. Pampering carries with it a materialistic bent. When you operate from that viewpoint, you are asking for trouble. I see so many kids today for whom a car has become a status symbol, a luxury to be flaunted, without which they seem incomplete.

When I was in high school, some time ago now, we managed. My folks did drop me off at school in the morning, but I always walked home after school, even with all my books and such. I didn't even give it a thought. It was one of the responsibilities of life. I went to school three miles from our home. Usually I was with friends, so it was a time of companionship, not some terrible ordeal.

Kids tend to expect a great deal and in return they try to give very little.

The Value of Responsibility

Commitment to responsibility must be learned, needs to be learned, along with discipline. It's all a part of the necessity of their doing their part in the home. I just see so many young people who have little or no responsibility. Activities outside the home may have their place but too often these become harmfully competitive. On Friday night there is usually an activity for them— and then all day Saturday there is often Little League or whatever—and, well, you see what I mean. These tend to come first and then responsibility at home gets shortchanged.

The Problem With Television

Television wasn't so much a factor in my childhood. I have never been a big fan of TV. I feel very strongly about its place in our home, which means that it has very little place actually. We carefully control what the kids watch. Usually it's limited to sports and not much else. I allow them to watch "Little House on the Prairie" because I think it's a wholesome program. It teaches good values, which so few other programs do these days. But the TV goes on only if their homework is done and all chores are completed.

Most of the time, though, I would prefer to have the children outside playing basketball or skating or whatever, or having them inside playing something creative like Scrabble or challenging like chess. TV is junk food for the mind, as someone said recently.

TV is nothing more than an escape for a lot of people. It's something to *occupy* their time. They fail to *redeem* the time, as the Bible urges us to do. Watching TV is easier than thinking or working. Look at "Soap," that Pearl Harbor mini-series. They all have something in them to justify sex on television, nudity, violence, and so forth. And then they say that these depictions don't begin, ever, to formulate the behavior of young people. Nonsense!

Christian School Education

The failure of public schools to educate children properly is a key consideration. With most public-school teachers there is a moral point of view that isn't consistent with the gospel. And, furthermore, there remains an appalling lack of interest in spiritual matters. It's a humanistic framework that dominates in public schools. This can be very, very destructive. That's why you're seeing the growth of Christian private schools that is apparent today—three such schools open each and every day, according to what I've heard.

But the government's going to try and step in as much as possible. If Christians don't get up and become actively heard, if they don't take up the cause of Christ and protest loudly, even Christian private schools won't be immune for very long.

Unwed Mothers

This whole problem was made so real to us just a short while ago. The head nurse at a nearby hospital was saying that the mother in question should keep the child, even though she's working full time and wouldn't have the regular contact with the baby that is so necessary. I pointed this and other considerations out to the nurse, but she said none of it makes any difference. All she could add was, "It can be done. I've seen it happen. It's done all the time."

But I told John, later, that the difference is the mother's a Christian. She's unselfish enough to want that child to be raised from the beginning in a strong Christian home where there is a father and an overall healthy environment.

There is simply no way that a girl who is twenty and unmarried and working and still interested in dating can give a child a proper environment. My idea of a home for a child involves more than merely feeding him and clothing him. Scriptural standards must be taught. The child must be prepared for life in the proper way, loving the Lord with all his heart and mind.

But that's not all: The nurse felt that if the girl didn't want to have the child, then rather than giving him up for adoption, the mother should have an abortion. I told her that that wasn't even an option. I said she is a Christian girl and she's going to do the right thing. What the nurse favored was so opposite to what every Christian mother should accept.

More kinds of child abuse exist than just the physical variety. Much of it can be emotional, psychological. The child would be neglected a good part of the time. It's better for her to give the child up if it's going to go into a strong Christian home.

Motion Pictures Today

My little niece went to see "Saturday Night Fever," and this concerns me. She's only fifteen years old. I think the question of going to movies or not going is a much more crucial question these days than several decades ago. Today you *expect* a lot of filth on screen—and you shouldn't go for that reason. It's often slipped in with a movie that otherwise seems perfectly proper.

We have a rule against movies with our children. We don't make a big thing of it. It's just that there is usually a priority that takes precedence at any given moment.

John and I have talked this over, and we are not going to make a practice of taking them. So much that is wholesome and entertaining exists apart from movies, and we find no compulsion to go.

The exception is that occasional Christian movie such as "The

Hiding Place." We enjoyed it very much. But just now our young-sters aren't old enough to appreciate all the ramifications of that picture . . . the heartache, the persecution.

You know even going to see a Christian movie in a secular theater is not a comfortable experience for me. That's my background, and John's. On the other hand we don't condemn this because the producers are reaching an element of the world that they wouldn't be otherwise. You'd never get these people into a church first.

Frankly, even allegedly Christian movies can fall short. A few months ago I saw one that had a great deal of offensive language in it—abusive language and some unnecessary scenes. It tried to appeal to both Christians and the unsaved, and was accepted by neither.

A Wife's Responsibility

You can't really be a good mother if you are a poor wife. The same worthwhile atmosphere that affects the children does so with the husband. I feel strongly about being a stabilizer in the home. I think our home should be a place where Johnny can come from all the burdens and pressures he faces and relax and feel protected. In a sense the home should be his refuge, his haven. It's a place where we are isolated from the world.

I work at this, I really do. I try to keep our home in such a manner that it is conducive to relaxation; that it is comfortable. I try to make meals that I know he will enjoy, as well as will the children. I try to please them. I try to have my days organized. And it's a full-time job with four children.

You know, I never get bored. I really love what I do. I enjoy baking. I have a lot of letter writing to do. And I handle a lot of phone calls at home. That's fine. I like being available to people. My main emphasis is the home. I don't go to retreats, at least not now. Oh, the day will come when my children will be grown, and they won't need me as they do now. But, you see, I feel the Lord has given me this family of mine, and every member of it deserves my first attention, my full responsibility.

Evelyn LeTourneau

When you're getting older, and you've lost someone very dear to you, you find yourself occasionally sitting back and reliving in memory moments experienced between the two of you. When the person involved happened to be R. G. LeTourneau, your husband, you do indeed have much to recall.

Such as the loss of your son Don.

"Don and I both left the airport at the same time but in different private planes," Evelyn told me. "He was going to North Carolina and I was going to Peoria, Illinois, then on to Winona Lake. Well, I made it to Peoria and had just finished eating dinner with my brother."

Don is dead!

Killed instantly.

"Did you have to identify the body, Evelyn?" I asked.

"No, my brother-in-law did. They wouldn't let us see it. That was the hardest part."

"Was there *any* problem with death denial? Did you say to

yourself, 'No, it couldn't be true'—or anything of the sort?''

"No, I really don't think so. I had begun to realize that there were a lot of things worse than death.

"But while I didn't go into denial, I did turn deathly sick, to be honest. I had just eaten my dinner and I lost it all in the bathroom.

"But the Lord gives you strength in the midst of your weakness. You say to yourself, as you reflect on the future, that if thus and such occurred, you don't know how you'd ever be able to face it. But the Lord doesn't promise you strength ahead of time. He promises it to you *when you need it*. It's a supernatural occurrence. How could I face that closed coffin? How could I stand there and know that my Don's earthly body was inside?''

The same body that had been Don's instrument of communication for his soul, his spirit, the body through which he spoke to her, laughed with her, cried with her. True, it was only a shell, but it was, after all, the physical manifestation of her son.

"I'm just a very mortal, helpless mother," she said. "Yet I had to attend my son's funeral, try to act brave, and even give a little speech to our friends afterwards. On my own I couldn't do it. Yet when I got to my feet and opened my mouth, the Lord provided the ability, the words. But this didn't happen until I got to my feet and *started* to speak, *not* before.''

And she faced death many years later when R. G. was dying.

"We were out in California with my brother," Evelyn recalled. "It was about 5:00 in the morning. He took with this bad convulsion, then another—one right after the other. We had to get an ambulance from about fifteen miles away. Then it was some seventeen or eighteen miles to the hospital. We brought him home in a week, and his mind wasn't too bad initially. He could function relatively normally.''

R. G. was eighty years old at the time. He would not live to be eighty-one. Everyone kind of suspected that this would be the case. There was very little denial within the family circle.

"I was returning from a convention at which I was named 'Texas Mother of the Year,' '' Evelyn recalled. "He had to wait for about forty-five minutes before the plane landed, and he had another stroke.''

When she disembarked there was a crowd at the airport. The high-school band was playing, and all the city officials were there, in addition to a crowd of spectators numbering a thousand or more. They had thrown a little red carpet out for her.

"I had a bouquet of roses presented to me. I just couldn't get away from them. They were all jammed around me. Then I had to go to the platform and give a speech."

During the time R. G. was waiting, the pain must have been severe, but he wouldn't let them take him home, or to the hospital. He had waited this long; he wasn't going to disappoint his beloved Evelyn.

"Finally, when I did break away and get to the car, awareness had left him. He didn't even know me. . . ."

He never said a word after that. The stroke had robbed him of the ability to speak. The last four weeks of his life were the roughest.

"I just watched him go down and down," she said, catching back a sob. Still there were tears, and she had to pause to wipe them away. "When he breathed that last breath, it was a relief. There was no more suffering for him, no more waiting by his side, helpless. All our married lives I had waited on him—picked out his clothes, helped him with his appointments, did so much for that man. I knew that if the Lord called me home first, he'd be lost without me. He couldn't have functioned. And, suddenly, he was dying, in so much pain, and there was nothing, absolutely nothing that I could do. He had to go on this journey alone."

The doctors and nurses were amazed at how well Evelyn held up in the midst of the ordeal. They were secretly saying, among themselves, that she would go all to pieces when he actually died.

He was home, in his own bed, when it happened. All the children were there except Roy who was scheduled to sing at church. He didn't want to go and preferred to stay at home, but Evelyn urged him to keep the commitment.

"Pop would want you to be there, honoring the Lord in song," she told her son.

He went ahead and sang as never before. . . .

That was in 1968.

Evelyn today is a little more tired. She needs a cane and a crutch in order to get around successfully from place to place. But she still drives, and she still makes speeches across the country. One suspects that she will continue to live this way until the last possible moment.

"Do you mind talking about R. G., the years you had with him?" I asked at one point.

"No," she said. "Forgive me, but my voice breaks sometimes."

Life is good now, not the same as when R. G. and she walked the campus, waving to the students, dreaming dreams of where the college would be heading in a few years, what new achievements were going to be added to an already hefty list. But she survives; she is happy. Young people continue to come to her for advice—and there are the family reunions.

"Oh, we get together and we have a ball," she said, her eyes twinkling. "Altogether this family has grown to fifty-three members! We get together at my son Ben's house. It's a huge, big house, and we share so much. But this has never been unusual. I came from a large family. So did my husband. We've always thrown parties for friends from church and business. My mother always entertained all the preachers in town. Nothing fancy, but we managed to make everybody happy."

Here, in their house on campus, the door was never locked. People were free to come and go. Evelyn and R. G. never kept themselves isolated from students or staff. What she had learned in family life helped in the lives of those at the college or in the business, those who would come to her for advice.

"Above all I encourage people—husbands and wives, parents and children, as well as good friends—to pray together. That's what Pop and I did. You can't stay mad at one another when you do this. You just kiss and make up, actually before you ever get up off your knees.

"I think it is also very important for people to listen to one another, especially mothers in raising their children. Take time to do this. Even if what the kids say seems frivolous to you, to them it may be something very, very crucial. Talk with them; pray with them; explain things to them. You are molding a human life, and this is more important than being President of the United States. It's basic to everything. Live what you preach. That's one thing our kids always said about Pop. They didn't agree with him all the time, but he was consistent and they respected him for this. He didn't say one thing and do something else.

"And wives have to get used to doing things for their husbands. I remember when Pop and I were in an automobile wreck in 1937. His joints were stiff as a result and he couldn't reach his feet easily. One of his legs swelled pretty badly. Furthermore, he had to wear elastic stockings on both legs. So I'd have to get up and pull his stockings on for him, and put his shoes on, and then hold his pants while he climbed into them. I used to scrub his back when he was in the tub; he enjoyed this—and I enjoyed making him feel good. It wasn't demeaning; I didn't lose any of my self-respect or dignity as a woman."

R. G. is buried right on the campus. There's a metal fence surrounding that plot of ground. Evelyn goes to the site often. She weeps, her mind recalling when he was with her, and they'd laugh together, cry together, experience *together* the good and the bad times.

Maybe, just maybe, what he wrote about her in his book, *Mover of Men and Mountains,* will also be recalled:

> With deep love and appreciation, I dedicate this book to my beloved partner and wife, Evelyn, who for over four decades has always been by my side to give me love, cooperation, and understanding when others doubted. Through the years she has joined me in mutual devotion and prayer to our Heavenly Father and has helped me keep faith when the vision of others was limited—truly a helpmate given by God.

Joyce Fasi

Just before leaving for an interview with Joyce Fasi, wife of Honolulu's mayor, I sat on the veranda of the Royal Hawaiian Hotel. I could see legendary Diamond Head to my left. It was partially obscured by high-rise hotels but enough of it remained visible to fill me with a little awe. My mind wandered back in time, trying to conjure up what the scene might have been like before statehood had opened the floodgates of development.

Directly in front of me was the astonishingly beautiful Pacific Ocean. Somehow around the Hawaiian islands this part of the Pacific is transformed. It is remarkably clear, and varied in color, with turquoise, aquamarine, navy blue, and other shades commingling in any given section.

To my right were tall, swaying palm trees. I could hear the branches "singing" an ancient Hawaiian melody, far more authentic than the scratchy phonograph records that piped in "atmosphere" along the bustling shopping vicinities of Ala Moana or Keemeauku.

A spell.

It calls. If you are an addict it beckons you again and again, and you never become bored. Your addiction is not one of drugs or alcohol but of an appreciation for the very special beauty of Hawaii; the just plain niceness of the inhabitants; the joy of driving through sugarcane fields and coming to the ocean which you see from a lookout point on a towering mountain.

Joyce Fasi lives in Honolulu as a permanent resident. That fact in itself means that she has much for which to be thankful. But along with the blessings there have been frustrations as a result of her husband's political career, particularly his current status as Honolulu's mayor.

"From the beginning he was the maverick," she said. "He was always the odd guy, doing things that the establishment didn't do or wasn't in favor of. The newspapers started reporting his actions, his decisions. When people couldn't get in touch with him, they got to me. Here I was, the mother of six children of our own, and the stepmother of Frank's five children from his previous marriage. I also had the responsibility of dealing with all those calls, including obscene calls, and vicious personal rumors."

"Did those children by his first wife accept you?" I asked.

"Well, it was difficult. I'd be lying if I said otherwise. I have to admit that, at the time, I was really not the best mother. I don't think I was the best stepmother either. I was letting a lot of things disturb me, and I'd sometimes take it out on the children. Don't misunderstand me, we have some wonderful memories. I really thought I was doing the best job as a mother, under the circumstances.

"Whenever I was upset I became a nagging, uptight mother, unfortunately. I couldn't take it out on my husband because he was gone most of each day, so I vented my emotions on the children. Not that I would beat up on them or abuse them, but, you know, I was a little harsher than I could have been, and maybe I wasn't as loving.

"If I had known the Lord early on, I would not have been as demanding as I was. I would have been more loving. I would have known the Lord had died at Calvary to achieve forgiveness of my sins. Then I wouldn't have had to fight the guilt that was also gnawing at me because of the way I sometimes treated the children. My tongue constantly got me into trouble—my pride caused me always to have the last word.

"I would have depended more on prayer. I would have gone to the Lord with my frustrations instead of taking them out on the children. And I would have realized the tremendously pivotal role a mother has. If she is not loving and supportive enough, then everything else falls apart."

Her own childhood certainly wasn't the steadiest in terms of providing the spiritual foundation that would have been such a help to her later on.

"I was born into a Buddhist family, with heavy Japanese orientation. My mother died when I was very young. I was raised by an older sister. Although she, too, was Buddhist, she always sent me to a Christian Sunday school that was close to where we lived."

A Buddhist who converts to being a Christian is sometimes ostracized from his/her family. But this didn't happen in Joyce's case. Inexplicably her Buddhist sister encouraged her participation in Christian Sunday-school activities.

"I thank her for this because, you know, I did hear the message there, all those years that I was growing up. The seed was planted."

(Joyce maintains good links with the Buddhist community even now. She has spoken at Buddhist temples, and professed her love for Jesus Christ. Never has she sensed opposition.)

But the seed didn't mature for a long time. In the process she failed to give the strength and stability needed by her very large family to survive in a political world.

What were the circumstances of her conversion?

"Actually I thought I already was a Christian. I considered myself one because of Sunday-school attendance and Bible-training school I went to when I was a teenager. I even sang in choirs. I always prayed before I went to bed and when I got up in the morning or before an exam. When I was in need, I always turned to the Lord. All this made me a Christian, in my own mind."

Let's summarize for a moment: Joyce was suddenly surrounded with the task of being stepmother to five children. Within six years of the wedding, six more children were added to the family circle. Piled on top of this were the phone calls, the absences on Frank's part because of his political career—and a "Christian" foundation that was never more than shifting sand instead of the rock that Joyce thought.

Little wonder that everything in her life was reaching a point of explosion and then total collapse.

"Fortunately someone in the community here was praying for me," Joyce said. "She was very persistent. She kept inviting me to Christian Women's Club luncheons. But I kept turning her down. I thought to myself, 'Oh, no, not another religious group.' I couldn't stand the thought. I always found an excuse not to go. I went bowling on Tuesdays, and I used to have my hair and my nails done that day. It was just a busy, busy day for me. I could never possibly include a luncheon as well. Here is where persistence in prayer for family and friends alike would pay off.

"This particular Tuesday I guess the Lord was really preparing me for it. She invited me again and I thought, 'Well, I'll accept this one time just to get her off my back. Maybe she won't bother me again if I do.'"

But the battle didn't end. Satan tried to stop her. She got to the hotel where the luncheon was being held, then nearly decided to pass it by. She was struggling, intensely, part of her not wanting to go in, the other hungry for the message she perceived would be given, a message of peace and joy.

"I decided that I really would attend it. I felt a little guilty about the possibility of backing out. I got there in time to hear the guest speaker, and was she dynamic! All I remember is that when she gave that invitation, calling for all those who were depressed and maybe frustrated, heavy-laden, to open their heart's door to Jesus, I did! And that was the real beginning of the meaningful part of my life, eight years ago. As a woman, I became more compassionate and understanding, and appreciated the inner person more than the outer trappings."

How her life did change! Not overnight. Christian books and films that give the impression of overnight transformation are terribly misleading. So often, in films, for example, we are given eighty-five minutes of the problem and five minutes of the solution. Unrealistic, to say the least. Conversion isn't some sanctified magic wand that we wave around and all of life's problems flee before it.

Nor was it this way with Joyce. The difference in her life was Christ. The other circumstances didn't change materially. What did change was Joyce's approach to them.

"I realized the irony of knowing that other people envied me even though my life was so confused before the Lord entered it," she told me. "I had nice clothes, a nice house and car, all the good materialistic embellishments. But they didn't realize what I was undergoing. So, in addition to everything else, I began to see how things hungry I was—how much of a sin that was and how it led to the sin of envy in others.

"I got into the Bible much, much more. I came to think of it as our service manual, our instructional manual for life. You don't invent something without a guide as to how to use that invention. God invented us, and He gave us His guide so that we can be functioning properly."

Joyce's life today is much more Christ-centered than before. I was discussing the Hawaiian trip with Joyce Landorf, and it turned out that she had met the other Joyce not long before. Joyce Landorf's comment was: "Your book will be that much richer for including her." So many others, including Cliff Scott of KAIM, the Billy Graham radio station in Honolulu, were equally praising of this pert, happy, candid woman.

But what about Frank?

There is some feeling in Hawaiian Christian circles that he's not made that all-important final commitment. That he is not, to use the current term, "born again" but is very close.

"When I learned to be a submissive wife, to put my family first, when I changed so much, well, you know, any man would see that. Right? At first, though, I forced the submission thing. It was difficult—I used to always have the last say in an argument and it was difficult for me to keep silent. But as I matured and grew in the Word, asking the Lord to help me handle my life, it got easier and easier. So many people would ask about the change in me.

"Then Frank and I started sharing our prayers which we hadn't done before. Frank started to change, too."

"But has he accepted Christ as Savior and Lord?" I asked.

"I feel that he has done so. He may not have professed his conversion in front of a whole group of people, but he has done it quietly. He has done it before the Lord, and that's really the most important step. He has frequently told *me* of his love for Christ and what Christ has done in his life. Frank admits being dependent upon the Lord for giving him direction during each day. But he has never felt it necessary to wear his faith on his sleeve. In other words, he would never want to use his Christianity in any political way.

"But, sometimes, when people come into his office, and unload so many problems, he tells them how much he relies on prayer. He asks them, 'Have you tried praying?' But to campaign partially on his faith, well, he'll never fall into that trap. That's why he holds back. People who know him really well know the truth about my husband."

Though Frank still manifests some weaknesses, he has conquered others.

"I've seen him overcome many, many of those," Joyce said. "For example: He used to be much more outspoken and very impatient with people. Now I feel that he is considerably more patient, sometimes more than I am. I think he is even more forgiving than I tend to be. It takes me longer to forgive certain people who have wronged us. Frank will catch this and throw it back at me by saying, 'Mommy, you call yourself a Christian?'

"I think we've both grown, and it had to start with me. Wives have that kind of influence with their husbands. When husbands see changes in their wives, changes that are inspired by their conversion to Christ, then they themselves become aware of God's presence to a greater extent than before."

But they have to be so careful about what they say. Vultures lurk in the political jungle, ready to tear them apart.

"Frank finished a final campaign speech by saying we would leave the results in God's hands—'That God's will be done' in our lives.

"Well, the newspapers used that against us with a headline that read, 'FASI HAS A DIRECT HOT LINE TO GOD.' We know this is Satan trying to get at us, trying to discourage us.

"You know, through these and other instances, I've seen my husband come home and often say, 'Praise the Lord! We're going to survive.' "

Another barometer reading of Joyce's spiritual condition is that she now prays for even the reporters, the newspaper editors who seem to be constantly at Frank's throat.

Frank is fifteen years older than Joyce. When he's seventy, she'll be only a vibrant fifty-five. Most people look at a situation such as this and say that it's too much of a gap. Joyce feels otherwise.

"My husband at fifty-eight now is a lot more active than many much younger people I know. I think a woman begins to feel, to act older earlier than does a man. Frank has often said, 'Mommy, if you were my age, there would be no way you could keep up with me.' Often, the woman is slowing down but the man is yet very active, energetic. God has gifted Frank with foresight, imagination, and a memory for facts, and the intelligence to put his ideas to work."

Permissiveness.

It bothers Joyce. And Frank. That more Christians aren't taking a stand against it—in the home, in business, in government—puzzles them.

"Frank stands against compromise in government when principles are involved," she said. "That is why the newspapers and special interest groups attack him. It would be so much easier for him to go along with the other guys. Then they'd leave him alone. But compromise does not make a wrong situation right. He says again and again, 'I'm going to stand up for what's right.' He will not bend his principles. He believes that honesty and loyalty are supremely important in people. One woman put it this way, 'Nobody likes Frank Fasi but the people.' "

"But his reputation is in the opposite direction," I pointed out frankly.

"Yes, I know, but this is where Satan can really get to a person who refuses to prostitute himself. Frank feels that the newspapers here have had an illegal monopoly for many, many years. In the past the powers that be have not wanted to change the situation due to the power of the newspapers. Frank has been saying that if they're going to have a monopoly, then they should be monitored by an organization like the PUC so that their rates and profits can be controlled. As it is, the newspapers raise their rates anytime they want, and nobody can do anything about it."

I was impressed by Joyce Fasi. As she spoke she was animated. She worked hard to give a good interview. I never got the idea that she was holding back, that she was exaggerating. We spent quite a bit of time together, and she appeared eager to answer any question I put to her.

As I drove away, down beautiful Makiki Street, I thought of one other part of the interview.

"More than twenty years ago Frank foresaw what would become of Waikiki if we all weren't careful," she had said. "He wanted them to start the hotels one block back from the beach, and use the land that the hotels now occupy as kind of park, keeping the natural beauty that you see on other parts of Oahu, as well as Maui and the other islands. But he couldn't convince anyone."

As I drove into the Waikiki area, I saw the massage parlor fronts that were springing up, the honky-tonk trinket stores, fast food places, and the striptease joints. Some palm trees lined the street as you came upon an old-time touch—an organ-grinder with his trained monkey, or a Hawaiian street singer who, in this case, was singing How Great Thou Art. But the main thoroughfare of decades ago had definitely deteriorated, sinking into the quicksand of commercial interests.

Developers are trying to tear up more of this paradise, ripping away the orchids, the palms, and the fruit trees in favor of more concrete, more artificiality, raping the wilderness of its natural allure.

Fighting this trend is a little like fighting the encroachments of Satan in the Christian life. But Joyce and Frank Fasi are determined, with God's help, to win the battle.

Vonette Bright

Bill Bright heads one of the largest Christian ministries in the world, Campus Crusade for Christ at Arrowhead Springs, San Bernardino, California.

Over the years not an awful lot has been written about his wife Vonette. Getting to interview her for this book was a special privilege. She is an attractive, energetic, sensible mother who has learned to adjust to the ever-increasing demands of a ministry that proposes to raise $1,000,000,000 for evangelism over the next five years.

Being a parent is fraught with difficulties. Today it is a far harder task to be a successful parent than it was just twenty-five years ago. Since parents are ordinary human beings with an extremely demanding job on their hands, you can be sure they won't do perfectly all that needs to be done. Where do you feel, Vonette, that parents, especially mothers, fail the most?

Requiring too much perfection is one of the most serious, in my opinion. A close second is not giving attention when attention is needed. Mothers often just have to drop everything at the moment a child needs them.

Another failure is that of being overly protective, not giving the child liberty enough to really express himself and then venture out a little on his own.

You have two children. Both are grown-up now—one is married. They apparently are well past the point of rebellion. But when rebellion did occur, how was it manifested?

We have been very fortunate. I would say that our oldest son, at the age of nineteen, exercised a degree of rebellion/ independence by getting his own apartment. We weren't quite ready for that, but it was his own choice.

How do you mean you weren't quite ready for him to do that?

Well, we would have just preferred that he stayed at home. But he wanted his own apartment and so he moved. It was at a time when he was trying to find himself. He wanted to make sure that his faith was *his* faith and not merely his parents.

In no way did he ever deny the Word. He wanted to apply it to his own life, in a way that he could totally accept. He was seeking fellowship, also, with people who really lived holy lives. You see, he was disappointed in what he saw in some Christians.

Bill is away often. How have you sought to minimize the negative impact this could have had upon the children?

We have felt called to the ministry as a family. How tragic when a man insists upon going into the ministry if his wife does not feel called. That's not been a problem with us. I was/am totally with Bill.

We recognized the difficulties from the beginning. We knew that it was impossible for Bill to give undivided attention to the children, but it was possible for me to do that.

Furthermore, I have made it a point of never criticizing their father when he was away or involved apart from the home. I never did this, even if I myself felt resentful from time to time. And there have been times when resentment has been felt, but I would talk it out with Bill, just the two of us away from the children.

There have been times when the children would come to me and say something like, 'Well, doesn't Daddy care for us?' And I'd

91

say, 'Of course your Daddy cares.' I would somehow alert Bill that pressure was building up, and it would work out that he would come in and take them on a picnic because they had a need for him at that particular time. He would be alone with them, giving them his undivided attention.

Bill has been a marvelous father in that he always told the children, 'Look, you come first.'

I remember when, on two or three occasions, our oldest son would go to the office, to be where his father was. Bill would say, 'Welcome. Come on in, Son. We're in the middle of a meeting. Why don't you sit with us?'

So he would sit for a little while and Bill would occasionally try to bring him into the conversation, saying, 'Now, Son, we're discussing such and such. What do you think about this?' Bill was always amazed because our boy would come out with an opinion that evidenced really mature judgment. But, sometimes, he wouldn't say anything. Soon he would get up, indicate that it was time for him to go. Just like that.

It was as if he were testing his dad, to see if he was really welcome in the meeting.

Another time, when he was a teenager, he had a flat tire downtown. He called Bill and said, 'Dad, I've got a flat. What should I do?' Bill replied, 'Just stay there. I'll be right over.' Zach still points out to people that his dad came. 'I had a flat,' he says, 'and Dad didn't send somebody else. He came himself.'

When someone such as Bill reaches rather notable status internationally, don't you think that it is possible that parenthood can be a hindrance? Doesn't Paul hint this at some point? That if you're not married you owe your allegiance only to the Lord, but, if you're married, the family comes first.

In our case I think being a family has enhanced the ministry. I'd hate to think what our lives would have been like apart from each other or apart from the children.

Being a mother has given me a compassion for others, an identification with millions of people. I think we're far better individuals because of our experience with the children. Our personalities have more dimension. We have a greater understanding of the fatherhood of God. We continually draw upon experiences with the children for sermons, for our writings, for simple conversation.

But I do feel that marriage can be a tremendous handicap if it's not a solid one. A family can hinder a ministry's accomplishments if that family's not pulling together, if they're not a unit. This is the tragedy I see so many times, this lack of togetherness. A man will not include his wife in the ministry as he should. Divisions occur. It's sad.

We have always operated *as* a family. Even when I was recuperating from surgery. Well, nothing has ever split us apart. Bill was so protective, so careful. Knowing I couldn't make a bed, he would do this first thing in the morning so that I wouldn't be even tempted to try. Or he would be very quick if he found the sink full of dishes to put them into the dishwasher.

Was the operation for cancer?

No. My condition could have developed that way, but it wasn't to do so, fortunately.

Did you feel better after the operation than you did before?

(Laughter)

I felt perfect before the operation!

I had no indication of anything being wrong. It was just that they found a tumor in the early stage that was growing very fast. They were able to catch it before it caused any problems.

I've learned to put all my trust in God. It's been a precious experience over the years. We can't prevent some things from happening in life. We just can't. There wasn't a thing I could have done to change the basic situation, so why fret about it? It was just as if I'd laid myself in His arms and He'd lovingly patted me and nurtured me and cared for me.

What else would you like to say to parents/mothers?

I think they should learn to be relaxed in raising their children. Learn to be natural before them, to *live* before them, to *be* exactly what they *profess* to be. I think this is so important. I learned, as a mother, that my kids were quick to pick up inconsistencies and confront me with them.

We have been an expressive family. We never separated into little corners by ourselves. We lived *together*. We grew up together in a very real sense.

Patti Lewis

Very little of life fits into neat, predictable, and acceptable little packages. Soon after conversion, some people begin to slide back into their "old ways," whether they be drinking or whatever. But, we say to ourselves, the joy, the glow of the salvation experience should preclude that. The recently redeemed should dedicate themselves totally to Him. Can their confession of faith really have been very deep or genuine if they continue in what they should indeed be rejecting?

Would it were so that accepting Christ as Savior and Lord guaranteed instant and prolonged devotion to Him, precluding all those nasty sinning ways to which we were once prone. But this just isn't ever to be the case here on planet earth.

Even for the minority, those for whom salvation is a vibrant, life-changing experience at its most radiant, sin does intrude. Sinless perfection may seem logical but it is not obtained this side of glory. Logic—that of being able to please the Lord every minute of every day after this wondrous redemption we have embraced—

gives way, tattered, bruised, and rendered useless, in the face of the temptations of our sinful nature and the victories those temptations succeed in obtaining even with the most mature of Christians.

Life A.D.—literally, *after* Christ—for babes in Him is a mixture of the comforting, the joyous, right along with the frustrating and the puzzling.

"Roger, I am a babe in Christ," Patti Lewis was saying in the living room of the Bel Air home she, Jerry, and the boys have lived in for many years. Her anxiety was obvious as she continued: "People expect too much of me. They expect me to have all the answers to all the theological questions, and I just don't."

Of course not. Babes can assimilate milk. Meat is not yet part of their diet. Patti is at the milk stage. And yet—.

"I don't speak in tongues," she said. "Does that mean I'm not born again?"

It happened in 1976. She accepted Christ into her life. He became her Savior, her Lord. There was the friend who had been praying for her for seven long years. And finally she made the jump.

But she's just in the growing stages now, the very early growing stages. Later will come maturity. She'll know. She'll feel when, no longer thinking as a child, Christian adulthood is just around the corner. There will be that hunger, that passion for learning more about Him, delving into His Word more fully.

"I'm still crawling, Roger," she continued. "I haven't come anywhere near my peak yet. I'm attending Bible-study classes and such, but I admit that I don't know my Bible like . . . well, those who are able to rattle off verses, having studied the Bible for so long. I'm still learning, you know, and it's very hard for me. When I say hard, it's because I am very busy with my family and other obligations. It seems, at times, as though everything is arrayed *against* my achieving a deeper Christain walk."

"Primarily your domestic and social obligations, Patti?" I asked.

"Not just that," she admitted.

The pressures. The people on all sides. Pulling at her. Expecting so much.

Like the time she and Jerry were doing a show with Oral Roberts and his wife Evelyn in North Carolina at Grandfather Mountain.

95

"It was so beautiful there," she recalled, her mind filling up with memories of the tall trees swaying in prevailing breezes, the scent of pine, the sound of birds, idyllic, peaceful. "I was visiting with Evelyn for awhile. Oral walks in and says, 'How are you?' We talked and he said, 'Shall we pray together?' So we held hands, the three of us. Oral is praying, Evelyn is praying, and they're speaking in tongues . . . Suddenly I start to tingle all over. Oral finishes praying and lets go of my hand. I say, 'Oral, please, my legs are so sore I can't stand.' I fall to my knees and stay there. Oral grabs my hands and Evelyn grabs me and we pray some more. He says, 'Let it out, let it out, Patti. You must let it out.' He wants me to speak in tongues. But it just wasn't coming out. I am so sore, my knees so weak. I am trying to *force* something that God supposedly gives freely."

Patti's husband is one of the most famous men in the world. He has been raised as a Jew all his life. Is he, now, a fulfilled Jew? Has he taken the same step that Patti did?

"Not yet," she admitted, "but he's getting close. He asks me questions, and he seems to be having a lot more peace than before. He's not yet born again, but soon, soon."

Jerry never insisted that their sons be raised as Jews.

"At the beginning he leaned toward this. Then when the rabbi came to the house and started talking, Jerry almost threw him out. 'I don't like your reformed Judaism. I prefer the old school. I don't want my son learning this . . . this stuff. It's so modern it has no personal meaning.' He is a very conservative man, and he'll be a very conservative fulfilled Jew when the Lord works in his life."

She added, "He's gotten many letters from fulfilled or completed Jews. He's fascinated by the whole idea. He'll read those letters with great interest."

And the children?

"They're like Jerry," she said, "but I think, in general, they may be a bit further along. We've joined hands and prayed. It makes me feel so good to share these moments with them."

"But they haven't made that leap of faith, of acceptance?"

"No, they haven't."

I speculated for a moment, asking Patti, "Now, let's say Chris became a born again/completed Jew, and a few months later he started dating a girl who was not saved, what would that do to you?"

"That wouldn't happen. I know my children. He'd look for

another completed Jew or a Christian. You see, these boys, they are so wonderful. All through the years they've liked very simple, very quiet, very nice young ladies. They've never dated anybody who is a daughter of a movie star or producer or anyone like that. They prefer stable girls because they themselves are stable.

"They don't go in for the disco scene or fancy parties. Do you know what they do, Roger? They bring their girl friends here. They watch television, or they run Jerry's films, or they sit up in a room with me and we talk or play a game of some sort. They have fun in their home. If they go out, it's to dinner or a movie. They're not wild drivers. They're very sensible. They like healthy things: Chris is a diver; Anthony is into photography; and so on."

The house is indeed filled with love. You can sense that, a certain quietness, serenity about it.

"I accept Jesus as my Savior, my Lord," Patti said. "And though the boys don't, as yet, they still love Him. We all love Jesus."

"I went to do the George Otis High Adventure show. Now Jim Bakker and Pat Robertson, others, they're all calling me to come on their programs. I don't want to do it. I've said what I've had to say on TV and that's it. I don't want them to make a special case out of me. I mean, all of a sudden, I'm up there as an example to millions . . . and I must get everything right in my life. How can I tell others what to do until everything is straightened out for me? To do so, now, to say 'I did this and I did that,' well, it would be hypocrisy."

But people just won't leave her alone.

"They call and say, 'The Lord wants you to do this, otherwise we wouldn't be calling you.' It's so calculating, so businesslike. Then there are all those secretaries and arrangements and all the rest. It's an institution, a business."

If you're famous, if you're Patti Lewis or B. J. Thomas, and if you've accepted Christ into your life, well, the world is at your feet, the Christian world, that is. People flock to you, expecting great words of spiritual wisdom to drop from your lips like manna from Heaven.

"What if you gave in, Patti," I pointed out, "and went on. What if they asked you a question and you answered it innocently but your answer was theologically wrong? You'd be dead. People would look at you and condemn you."

"True. I realize that. It just frightens me. I tell them no, but you can be sure that, in another month or so, they'll call me again and insist that God wants me to go on their program. Like the time I was turning one of the secretaries down, telling her I just couldn't, and she said, 'Let's pray about it.' I thought, well, she's trying to twist my arm, or maybe God's, and it just didn't seem right."

Until some coverage in 1978, most people didn't realize that Jerry Lewis has had a physical nightmare for many years.

"Even today he is not free of pain," Patti remarked. "But it's bearable pain. He doesn't really suffer like he used to suffer."

More than a decade ago he fell onstage during a stunt.

"That particular fall really hurt him," she said. "He had been taking falls all his life, but that one really triggered everything. That's when all the trouble started. He learned to live with it all those years, but to do so he had to get involved with pills. It started with one pill, then more pills, and then, you know, it just got worse. His neck was/is in really bad shape.

"I know what he went through. I know better than anybody else because he didn't sleep well at night. When he ached, I rubbed him as best I could, trying to help my husband. I never, never, never gave up hope that one day he would feel better.

"He did the telethon in 1978, and afterwards he started having pains in his neck, his stomach, everywhere. Each year there was trouble during and after the telethon. He had to have a shot of xylocaine each time in order for him to be able to finish.

"But that last telethon, he was so bad that we both knew he'd have to go to his friend and doctor Michael DeBakey in Houston for treatment. Well, they discovered that he had a gastric ulcer caused by all the medication for his neck. They treated him, which included keeping him asleep for five full days. That's the only way you can tie Jerry down.

"I sat in that hospital room for those days. They woke him up, briefly, just to eat. Five days later he was released. They had cleaned him out, driven the medicine from his system. Dr. DeBakey told him, 'Now, I'm giving you a new medication that is not addictive.' He paused then added, 'Don't take it unless you really have to.' Months went by and Jerry didn't need a pill at all, but he wasn't pain free. As I said, he's certainly a lot better today.

"Roger, it's almost unfathomable for the rest of us to imagine living with pain, to a greater or lesser intensity, every day of our life. The cold affects him. Being over tired does, too. So many things can kick off a pain spell."

Patti, is there anything you could not forgive as far as your sons are concerned?

"I would be close to that if they showed that they did not have a respect and a love for humanity. I have great sympathy for people. So does my husband. And I think our children are the same way.

"Insensitive people bother me. If somebody needs help, and you can possibly give it, I don't think that help should be held back. I mean, I saw a woman pushing a basket in a market and it was heavy for her. I started to help her. She looked at me, as though to say, 'What are you doing?' She must have thought I was trying to take it away from her. I said, 'I'm just helping you because you are having trouble.' She was so relieved."

The paranoia that is forced upon us by social conditions is upsetting to realize.

Your children seem to be very happy, well-adjusted. Was your childhood as stable?

"No, it wasn't, Roger. I remember when I was a little girl my mother and father were divorced. My father took us and boarded us on farms and what-have-you. My mother went to Detroit and got married again. It was a rough time for me."

Have any of your sons had a rough time of it in any way?

"Only Gary, because he met this girl and just wanted to marry her so badly. That was one I couldn't do anything about. Shortly after he was drafted and sent to Korea. She had a baby while he was in the service, and he wasn't ready for all the responsibility.

"Poor Gary. They all were smoking pot. He said, 'Mother, there are rats the size of big cats, and they wait to lunge at our food or at us.' When he came back this poor kid was lost. The musical styles changed; the band had broken up; and he was just . . . just floundering something awful. His first marriage broke up, and he got into trouble a couple of times.

"But he came out of it. He remarried. He's found a really nice lady this time."

Patti and I talked for quite a while longer. She told me of her love for the Lord, of His place in her life, of her gratitude to Him for many, many blessings.

Does she know Christ as Savior and Lord? That much seems apparent. I found out about her conversion through a friend of a friend. She was convinced of Patti's genuineness and, after spending some time with her, so am I.

If she can free herself of the doubts, the frustrations that others are forcing upon her, then I think the Holy Spirit will make her a powerful witness, a woman who could be His instrument in bringing to Christ a man who has had influence with millions of people over the years, a man whose heart is good, whose concern is for others.

When we are dealing with a real baby, a physical baby, we don't push him/her too far. We take him/her by stages. It would be stupidity, cruel and inhuman, to expect, to *force* that baby to walk before he/she is ready.

Thus it is with a spiritual babe. Countless numbers have been turned off by people pulling at them, demanding this and that. *Forcing* them into behavior for which they aren't ready, may never be ready, and, worst of all, which may not even be valid behavior in the first place.

I left the Lewis house that day with a vivid picture in my mind, a scene that has been played in memory several times since. It was a picture of a woman wanting to grow in Christ, a woman who has "experienced salvation" and whose whole outlook on life is changing, yet a woman who felt it necessary to look at me, tears visible in her eyes as she asked, "Roger, I don't speak in tongues. Does that mean I'm not born again?"

Shirley Dobson

Q. When you became Mrs. James Dobson, did you find that married life required you to make a difficult personal adjustment?

A. There is always a period of adjustment in the early days of marriage. We had to learn to cooperate and compromise during our first year together. I was especially unprepared for the heavy responsibilities associated with teaching school and maintaining an apartment, with very little "free" time to myself. However, my marriage to Jim has been blessed by God right from the beginning. We have loved each other for twenty years, and there has never been a day when I've regretted marrying him. We never went through the earthshaking kind of conflicts that threaten to destroy so many marriages.

Q. You said you were unprepared for certain aspects of marriage. What did you mean?

A. Well, my early home life was pretty difficult. My father was an alcoholic, with all that condition implies for a family. We lived in poverty. I was never able to invite my friends to spend the night for fear that my dad would come home drunk. Only the children of alcoholics will understand how this affects a person. Consequently, we never had the kind of father-daughter relationship that is so important in a girl's life. This meant that Jim and I had to carve out our relationship without my having had a strong masculine figure to admire and follow during the formation years.

Q. Did your parents stay together?

A. No. Their relationship grew more and more strained, until my mother finally divorced my dad when I was in the sixth grade. That was the most important turning point for me, because my mother knew she was unable to raise two children alone. Even though she was not a committed Christian at the time, she believed in God and required my brother and me to attend a little neighborhood church. I was introduced to Jesus Christ there, and that experience spared me the deep emotional scars I might have borne from those years.

Q. How did becoming a Christian protect you?

A. Well, I learned to pray as a small child and developed a personal relationship with God. I remember getting on my knees and asking God for two favors at that time. First, that He would send us a Christian father who would take care of our family. A year later my mother married a wonderful man who later became a Christian. He met our financial needs and eventually even helped my brother and me through college. This was a fantastic answer to prayer, and I'm thankful to God for sending my stepfather to us. He and my mother are now members of a strong evangelical church near their home.

Secondly, I began praying (at only eleven years of age) that the Lord would someday guide me to a Christian husband who would give me the kind of home and stability I'd never had. God answered that prayer in the person of Jim. Contrary to my stormy childhood, Jim's early years were almost idyllic. He had a secure and loving home, which is undoubtedly why he has such a healthy outlook on life today. The Lord knew that I needed him.

102

Q. Have you found it difficult to subjugate your ambition and career opportunities to be a wife and mother?

A. No. I've never been ambitious in that way. I quit teaching after our first child was born, and I've never looked back. I am a part of Jim's ministry, and my responsibilities of wife and mother are all I want or can handle at this time. However, I am a very strong-willed person, and I tested Jim's leadership during the early years. I wanted him to lead our family, but I made him earn the right to lead it. He was a strong personality and prevailed in those struggles. However, he consistently treated me with respect and love, which made me feel comfortable in following him.

Q. What would have happened if you had married a passive, easygoing husband?

A. The relationship would have been in trouble from the beginning. I know I would have henpecked him to pieces. Like a lot of women, I needed a man who loved me but was stronger than I.

Q. Even the "beautiful people" seem to feel isolated and unloved today. Why do you think that is true?

A. Loneliness can touch everyone. A hundred years ago women would cook together, can together, have babies together, and grow old together. Now we live in isolation in our beautiful homes . . . having our beautiful hair fixed each week . . . and driving our beautiful cars. But what women really need is for someone to say, "I need you; I respect you; I will pray for you; I will be your friend." Beauty alone will not buy that kind of human interaction.

Q. A family can satisfy some of those emotional needs for its members. What suggestions do you have for making family life meaningful?

A. We've found that *traditions* can contribute immeasurably. They give a family a sense of identity and a mark of distinctiveness that satisfies a need for belonging in each of us. Our family has focused on many traditions that have become meaningful to us. We eat special foods, for example, on each holiday: it's turkey at Thanksgiving and Christmas; we have a southern dish of red beans and ham on New Year's Day; on the fourth of July we cook barbecued hamburgers, etc. We also weave Scripture and prayer into some of those occasions. This is especially important to me, because we had no traditions in my early homelife.

Q. What do you think about the effect of television on the family?

A. I believe it is destroying us. T.V. robs our time and teaches us atheistic values that undermine the home. I think we would be better off without television, but Jim and I have not yet made the decision to sell our sets.

Q. How would you summarize your own home and family, now? What are your long and short-term goals?

A. Jim and I see our friends (and his counselees) going through awful conflicts and divorce. We continually thank God that He has blessed and protected our relationship. I am confident of one thing. Our commitment to one another is *permanent;* it will survive until the Lord chooses to take one of us to Heaven.

As for our children, we have one overriding purpose which outweighs every other objective. That is to prepare them for a life of service to Jesus Christ. If we fail there, we fail! No other accomplishment will matter if we are unsuccessful in introducing them to the Christian way of life. They are the only "possessions" we can take to Heaven with us, and that is the supreme purpose in our home. We are asking God to answer this one prayer above all others.

If I can make one final comment, I want to thank the Lord for His leadership in my life. To imagine that the Creator of the universe heard the prayers of a little girl who had no status . . . no respect . . . nothing to give in return. He not only heard me pray in those dark moments, but He reached down and touched me and gave me the beautiful life I enjoy with Jim today. I just wish I could share that love with everybody who is going through difficult family experiences. The same God is available to everyone.

Laura Lee Oldham

Years ago I interviewed an actor named Robert Middleton. He was a huge man, well over three hundred pounds. On television and in the movies he played mostly villains, for he could look menacing indeed. But I found Bob to be a pleasant, sensitive, kind man whose personality belied his frequent acting roles.

"I've done a great deal for which I am thankful," he said, his deep voice adding emphasis. "But, you know, all these years of my life, I've had pain of one sort or another: the pain of rejection when I was younger, my peers taunting me because of my size; the physical pain I've experienced; so much more. To live to the age that I have, and yet find that I feel like crying more often than I feel like rejoicing, well, you wonder if the good times that do come about are really enough to sustain you."

I remember those moments vividly. An article for a national magazine resulted. In it I compared Bob to the circus clown who entertains thousands of people a year but whose heart is breaking beneath the garish costumes and the painted face.

I was struck by the similarities between Bob Middleton and Doug Oldham as I sat in the living room of the Oldham home at Franklin, Tennessee. Across from me was Laura Lee, his wife. She was telling the story of the troubled years of their marriage and, also, the physical circumstances that made life so rough for Doug.

"Doug doesn't just live life, he feels life. He has the true artist personality. He's sensitive, emotional. He needs a great deal of love. Since the Lord took over in our lives, we all have changed. But it wasn't until last year that Doug began to feel really good, happy, physically better.

"When we got married, we were kids. We weren't ready for married life. And Doug wasn't ready to earn a living. I was twenty, and he was twenty-one. Most of our problems came from just plain immaturity.

"There's a lot of talk today about people taking drugs for one reason or another. Well, Doug was taking Dexedrine before you heard much about it. He took it to lose weight. People now know that taking Dexedrine makes a living nut out of you. We didn't know that. Nobody knew much about it at that stage, and his emotional stability suffered as a result.

"Until last year, when he got on a diabetic diet, he always felt so bad. Even after our marriage got straightened out, he continued physically in a poor way. I remember how hard it was for Doug, at the age of twenty-two, to get up out of a chair and go from here to the kitchen and do something. He would have to say to himself, 'I must do it. I don't feel like doing it, but I must do it.' "

We take for granted such a simple act, standing up and walking to the kitchen. How many times a day do we do this? It is a part of life. We think nothing of it. But for Doug it required a conscious *decision*. Accompanying that was a high degree of real discomfort, even pain.

"It hurt to get up," Laura Lee continued, "and his skin was so sensitive. Here he was, needing love, yet when I put my arms around him in bed, he would react in pain.

"We don't know, even today, what caused this. When the body's out of balance, anything can happen. Really, when you think about Doug, he's phenomenal. He has done what he's done with his life, fighting every step of the way, and never—inside—feeling like doing anything at all.

"He had black, black moods—awful moods. He had gone down that spiral of emotional trauma so long that he was suicidal.

For years, after we were married, he was that way. Every little while he was threatening suicide—and this panicked me at first. Then I got angry. So you see both of us had a hand in the deterioration. At the age of thirty we were destroyed. And our girls had been living in the midst of a troubled situation during those early, formative years."

"How much did they perceive, really?" I asked.

"A great deal actually. Children are extremely sensitive to emotional anxiety between the parents. Doug tended to be harsh with them when he was in a depressed mood. I was caught in the role of alternately trying to protect my husband while protecting my children. All this crazy strain left me so emotionally drained that I had no time to feel good even about sitting and reading or praying with them.

"When the break finally came, and I truly believe that was in the Lord's timing, Doug was wonderfully and miraculous saved, actually saved from himself. About the only virtue I had, if you can call it that at this point, was that I was afraid not to trust the Lord. I was afraid not to give the Lord a chance to prove that He could change a life.

"To my surprise the Lord brought things around full circle and wrapped it all up in a special package! Instead of a hard and irritable person, Doug became the gentlest, kindest, most loving person anyone could ever live with! In retrospect, we now see that God is economical; He uses everything. Our weaknesses become strengths under His tutelage. The very person who had suffered because of his sensitive nature, in an unredeemed state, was now rejoicing because the Lord could use that sensitivity in a special way to help him feel the hurts and losses of other people.

"There is glory in the cross!

"There is something real and deep about understanding and sharing suffering. It is one of the great mysteries of the Christian life. Every Christian must come to some knowledge of the cross, and then the glory is there!

"So today all my friends envy me because Doug is such a thoughtful, loving person. He's the best husband and father in the world; he truly is!

"He's a friend to so many people. He does those nice things for people that most men think is foreign to their nature. It's innate, now, in Doug's. He puts more of himself out to somebody; does something so sweet that makes you feel needed and loved and

107

important. People like Doug are either great in human relations or extremely poor—and he's become great.

"The kids really love him. They all do things for him that just surprise me, things that most girls wouldn't do for a father. When he was leaving on a plane the other day, DeeDee was out with a friend. It was a stormy day and we were late leaving here to get to the airport. When we finally arrived, she had been sitting there for an hour, waiting, just to say good-bye to her daddy. He leaves town every week. It's not an unusual happening. Most nineteen-year-olds aren't willing to leave a friend in order to do that.

"Karen is a teacher in Virginia. She will miss two nights of sleep, and face a Monday-morning class of first graders with bleary eyes, to go with her daddy on the bus for a weekend of concerts.

"Paula is married with a little girl and lives in our town. She will make sure she's there to 'take care of Dad,' if I happen to be out of town. You can't buy or legislate that kind of love."

Often people who live with the disturbing, unpredictable, angry side of their personalities become, after they have been changed, even *better* family members than people who have a nice, calm, easygoing way about them—who have never encountered the emotinal problems of someone like Doug Oldham. It's as though the chaos rips away pretense and gets, ultimately, to the nucleus underneath. The Bible has much to say about tribulation working patience, and patience working faith. Would Joseph have been the man he became if he had not been abandoned by his brothers and gone through the initial hard times in Egypt? A refining process is necessary with many of us, taking away the veneer, the facade, and revealing what we are *genuinely* like or what we *can* genuinely be if we allow the Lord control of our lives.

"I think it's true," Laura Lee agreed. "In the first place, you try a lot harder. I mean, when Doug was, shall we say, transformed, and had command of himself, he tried hard and with great success. He didn't sort of slop along. He did his very best, whether he physically felt like it or not. That trying begins to pay off sooner or later. Doug said, at one point, 'I'm going to make this thing work, you know.'

"In retrospect, however, we realize Doug's new psychological outlook could have been hampered by his old physical problems.

The latter didn't change one bit. His body was being battered every day. He had to travel so much and be away from me and the kids. He had to fight the loneliness, together with the physical discomfort, and still hang on to his new outlook.

"He did it all by himself those first few years. His own booking. Driving his own car. Unloading and reloading his own equipment. It was years before he even had a piano player. All this is okay if you're a big, strong guy and you feel wonderful. But if you feel bad all the time, sometimes doing nightly concerts, driving all day and all night, yet have to appear happy and relaxed in front of hundreds, maybe thousands of people, it's horrendous for sure."

Life is different now. The early struggles and financial pinch have given way to a bit more security. There is less strain though there is still the travel, the long hours, the tiredness. But the Oldhams are solidly a happy family. That is a miracle considering what ashes this phoenix arose from.

Even so, as Paul who had a thorn in his flesh that the Lord apparently never totally removed, Laura Lee and Doug must yet face, from time to time, moments when life is hard and Doug doesn't feel good.

"But," says Laura Lee, "that is not what is vitally important. What is important is that, 'There is peace in the midst of the storm,' as a song by Steve Adams, Doug's pianist, says. And, 'We will glory in the cross,' as a song by Dottie Rambo says. Jesus is with us, making use of the negatives, turning them into positives. That is the true glory of the Christian life; peace in the storm, joy in sorrow. Thank God for this miraculous mystery. And we thank Him that He lets us live it day by day."

Betty Criswell

Struggling to Find the Lord

I feel sorry for anyone who has had to struggle in order to find the Lord. I don't think that this is the ideal way to salvation by any means. I think you may have a sensational testimony, and all of that may *sound* good, but I am sorry for the person who has to undergo that. I think your life is much better if you haven't had such experiences. There are always scars left, many of which the person involved may not be aware of. Others may feel differently, but, in my own experience, I haven't known the struggling part to forge any stronger a faith. I've never shook my fist at God and demanded,"Why have You done this to me?" I've accepted His will completely, without question.

The Activity Syndrome

Sometimes I think I do make the mistake of getting involved in too many activities, in and out of the church. It's draining. You tend to spin your wheels without really accomplishing very much. I can't do everything that people like to expect of me. I can't attend every meeting. I've had to learn to say no, but not as often as I should.

Influence and Testimony

The most powerful thing you possess is your influence, your testimony. I know some people who spend a great deal of the day watching soap operas. Well, I suppose there's nothing wrong in watching soap operas, but look at the time and energy you spend doing this. You could be doing something constructive, and something wonderful and helpful.

Furthermore, it may be harmless for you to go and see a good movie. But it all depends upon the sphere of your life—where you want it to be headed. Is that the best use of your influence? Because when you go, you will invariably influence others to follow your lead. I think if people saw my husband and me frequenting the movies, it would be harmful, hurtful all around. So we don't go.

A Difficult Choice

Our daughter wanted to sing professionally. She could have succeeded in the operatic field. She has a marvelous voice. She struggled with choosing between singing for the Lord and singing for the world. She didn't know what to do, and I think there were many times she felt God just left her completely alone.

Now I know that there are people who decide that they can be a better influence by entering worldly music, but our daughter decided against this. She thought since the Lord gave her the gift of such a fine voice she should use it entirely for Him.

Life's Regrets

Any regrets? Is there anybody who doesn't have regrets? Right now I feel I am doing more of what God wants me to do in Bible teaching. I regret not doing so earlier. Years ago we had a graded program in Sunday school. I was teaching a class of women, and there were problems. My husband and I talked about the matter. He said he believed it was best for me not to teach, because you can't say to a person, "You're not the age for me. Therefore you have to go to another class." I wasn't to teach again for a good while.

I think we made a mistake there, maybe, because that's the thing God has laid on my heart to do. I realize this now, and He has since blessed me as a result of my return to teaching. God just makes our class of 620 go and go and go. It's getting bigger all the time.

God told me the reason I was miserable was that I wasn't teaching. I was floundering around in organizational work.

An Unusual Life

My life has been unusual. My husband is a very busy, capable man. It just seemed that we were always doing *something*. After we had our daughter, we just didn't plan to have another child. It's as simple as that. It wasn't, we felt, God's purpose for us to raise a large family. There is no other man in the world who could do what my husband's doing. The added responsibility of *more* children couldn't have been handled with great effectiveness. Anyone who brings children into the world simply to boast of having a large family isn't really very interested in the welfare of those youngsters. Our attitude had nothing to do with any concern about the sort of world into which we'd launch a large family. I think you are limiting God's power to help young people when you say that the world is so bad we shouldn't give life to more children.

Married Too Young

Our daughter unfortunately did get married too young. That was a tragedy. Today she's married again, to the greatest man she could have found. He is one of the most glorious Christians I've ever known. He's an oral surgeon here in Dallas, as well as a concert pianist.

Did the divorce bother us? Of course it did. It was not in the heart of God that divorce should ever be. It was God's plan that there would be one man for one woman, permanently. That's the ideal. That's what God wanted. But He allowed divorce because man's sinful nature made it necessary from time to time. Ever since Eden His ideal has been thwarted by man's rebellion.

There is a great deal of talk about physical adultery, and rightly so. But there's such a thing as spiritual adultery—

Anita Bryant

Marion Lindsell

Jeanette Myra

Carole Carlson

Edith Schaeffer

Joyce Landorf

Joann Letherer

Beverly LaHaye

Ruth Narramore

Anne Kennedy

Berdyne Floren

destroying the spirit of a person, trying to completely break that spirit. It was a terrible thing for Ann. She was so young, as I've said, and he was a young minister who just lost his way. Everything possible was done by my husband to mend it, but it was like plowing water. Nothing could be done. I think Ann had every reason, Scripturally, to get a divorce. The union had been broken long before the divorce.

There was a child, and we reared that baby. Why did my husband and I do this rather than Ann herself? Well, she was a very young girl. We wanted her to go back to school. We wanted her to rebuild her life. Because of her music, she had to travel a bit. She wouldn't have been able to spend the time with her son that she should have. For his sake there needed to be stability in the home. He needed to grow up in a normal situation, with a mother and a daddy.

Ann's son was aware, from the time he began to understand some of the world around him, that we weren't his real parents—that Ann was indeed his mother. Everyone in the church knew also. We live in a fishbowl, my dear, and anyone is aware of anything in our life.

There are times when we could hope for more privacy, but we love to be with people. We love to share things with them. And I think God allowed this to come into our lives so that we might be more compassionate and less judgmental. Because today it is just so prevalent in so many homes. Now, whenever we run across it, particularly in a counseling situation, we can identify, we can sympathize more perceptively.

A minister and his wife are human sponges. We have our own problems, and we also soak up the problems of thousands of people in our congregation. By ourselves we simply couldn't endure. The strain would be too great. I hurt with people. We both do. There are times when you feel almost as deeply about their problems as about your own. There are times when you say to yourself, to each other, that this is all you can possibly take. I've heard my husband say that there are times when he feels he needs a pastor.

Are there people he turns to? The answer is no. He just feels that this is not what he should do. He is convinced that it is best for him not to be terribly close to any one person in the church. It's important to both of us that we remain true to the life-style that God has convicted us about.

Edith Schaeffer

Most people who read *L'Abri* by Edith Schaeffer have yearned to visit that community of the same name. Many do realize that dream and experience a real blessing, not only from fellowship with Edith and Francis, but also being in the majestic country where *L'Abri* is located, a country those two have loved for years.

Driving across Switzerland is an experience not equaled in any other place. Only there can you enjoy the mountain vistas, wonderful valleys, mixture of cultures—French, German, Austrian, Italian, and Swiss—and other riches that this remarkable spot offers.

I rented a car in Zurich, and my mother and I began a journey from there to Geneva, east to west. We stopped overnight in Lucerne where we had booked rooms at the Chateau Gutsch, a centuries-old authentic castle on a mountainside overlooking Lake Lucerne. The next morning we looked, stunned, at the panorama before us—early mist giving way under the invading rays of a bright sun; a city rising up from the mist almost as though it were being "born" just then; the old, old covered bridge that spans the lake; the twisting, winding streets, cobble-stoned mostly, lined by often quaint shops; the odor of baked goods drifting through the air. Later we strolled through Lucerne.

When we wound our way through valleys, up mountain roads, that in weather different from the autumn perfection we encountered would be tricky to put it mildly, we stopped often, just standing there in the open, looking upward, dwarfed in every way by the wonders of God's architecture.

On schedule, we managed to find our way to Huemoz, near Geneva. We checked in at a mountainside hotel, and then I called the Schaeffer residence. Edith answered and suggested that we might want to join a group for dinner. I indicated that we'd be right over.

The group Edith mentioned proved to be at least twenty strong, mostly college-age young people, both men and women. Edith introduced me to them briefly, and I went aside with Francis and talked about young people in general. (Dinner was not to begin for some time, and my mother happily got involved with Edith in the kitchen.)

Francis and I discussed why so many of the young were flocking to L'Abri.

"Isn't it true that much of evangelical or fundamental Christianity somehow tends to be anti-intellectual?" I suggested, feeling a little like a dwarf who was having a conversation about height with a giant.

"Yes, that's true," he replied. "I do believe that intellectualism has been shortchanged, and the richness of Christianity restricted, by not indicating the fact that the Bible deals with the whole spectrum of life—to the intellectual man and the educated man, as well as the middle-class man and others on planet earth."

"Is there anything inherently antithetical between fundamentalism and intellectualism, for example?" I asked.

"Of course not. In fact, I feel that real Biblical Christianity has the only answers, the only meaningful and lasting answers to the deep intellectual questions of this or any age."

And so they come, the young people, those with questions of the mind, those who feel that L'Abri is their last hope lest they turn from intellectual Christianity to intellectual humanistic philosophy. . . .

115

"It concerns me," Edith was saying in her suite near Los Angeles International Airport. "I think young people asking very honest questions have been affronted, baffled, assaulted, and at times destroyed by being told, when it comes to religion, that they must not ask questions. They must either sit cross-legged and smell the incense and meditate with an emptied mind, or go off into a dither of spiritual feeling, or have some push-button spiritual happening take place, or go off to church without questioning.

"And this is leading to suicide. I think even Christians can commit suicide in a moment of anger, in a moment of despair."

To many of us that seems incomprehensible. Whatever happened to the peace that passes all understanding? Or what about God not allowing us to be tempted or tested above that which we are able to endure?

Do young people who take their own lives go to Heaven? Are they engaging in an unpardonable sin? Or does God's forgiveness extend yet to this point?

"Of course they'll go to Heaven if they are Christians!" Edith declared. "But that doesn't negate the sin. It's wrong to commit suicide. There are so many mothers, so many fathers, whose sons or daughters have gone this route and who may be thinking that their youngsters are in some kind of eternal agony now as a result, punished by God for this sin. But if we assume that suicide is at the top of a long list of sins, that God would set aside the significance of Calvary for this or any other sin, well, we are saying the plan of salvation was either incomplete, not covering all contingencies, or that it is applied selectively, instead of being for all who accept Him as Savior and Lord."

But are suicides rewarded equally with, say, a Merrill Womach who has undergone so much suffering? If there were *ever* justification for suicide, he would have it.

"I don't think anybody is rewarded equally," she said, "no more than we as mothers treat our children equally. We cannot. We are different year by year. So are they, and our children are not all born on the same day, unless we do have quintuplets.

"The diversity of creation, the marvel of it, is that there is a real specialness in my not being just like you, and having totally different talents, but complementing each other. The same is true of husband/wife relationships. Equality would rob the wonder of what is to be there if two persons are woven together with totally diverse personalities, different strengths and weaknesses.

"In Heaven a woman spending twenty-five years in a remote Chinese prison may be winning greater victories and living closer to the Lord than some who are hailed as the greatest Christians in history. God who is our judge has a different perspective and perfect knowledge. We have a Giver of rewards who is guided by perfect justice."

* * * * *

"Hi, Priscilla," I said over the phone receiver.

"I'm ready now," replied Priscilla Schaeffer Sandri.

The conversation with Priscilla covered a great deal of territory. Virtually all of it had, as a foundation, discussion of influences affecting parents as well as young people in an age that is probably one of the most turbulent in history.

"Do you think a lot of individuality is being lost today?" I asked.

"Oh, yes! No question in my mind. On one side you have the terrible danger of your individuality being lost. On the other, you have the great hurt that people feel as a result. So what happens is a frantic, mad, seeking after identity: Who am I? Where am I needed? What am I here for? Whether it be from the extreme feminists groups blaming everything on men, or whether it be from other individuals, masculine as well as feminine, the cry is one of people losing *themselves* in our culture."

"How are you encouraging individuality in your children?"

"It began for John and me from the moment each came into the world. We realized that each child was/is a separate being. My first two were very close together, and yet they're as different as night and day. I'm getting absolutely opposite results from them.

"Motherhood came, for me, at a time when I was struggling through learning to accept and appreciate my husband: Who he was and just what he meant in the relationship. I saw significant parallels between the lessons I learned in this perspective and how I should approach my role as mother. I cannot take my husband and then remake him, putting together in a different formation all the bits and pieces of himself, making him into the image of what I think he should be.

"I can't do that with my children, either. Yes, we mothers have the duty of caring for and disciplining our youngsters and guiding them. But we mustn't suffocate them; we mustn't dictate their *personalities*.

117

"I feel that we as image bearers of God have a very special calling to be parents who show the love of God, the Fatherhood of God in the proper light. When He deals personally with His people throughout the Bible as well as subsequent history, He takes much into consideration: the person involved; the historic moment. He's taking each individual person and He's speaking to each separately.

"I feel that we as Christian parents come to our children with no easy one, two, three ways of discipline, that each child requires a somewhat different perspective. What is very important is for us to realize that we have the responsibility in some small, poor way to be image bearers, showing them as time passes what God wants them to see through us.

"I have been terribly honest with them as to who *I* am. I will give them warning if I am at the end of my tether and really very tired, and can't take very much more. I say, 'Now, listen, Mommy is really nervous; she's frustrated; and so Mommy is going to probably be angry if you don't leave her alone just now.'

"You try to warn them when you feel an explosion is coming on. You try to be candid about how you feel, and why you feel that way, so they can be prepared when you let loose with your anger. You become a human being with them, given to weaknesses just as they are."

* * * * *

Edith and I were talking about the notion, prevalent in some Christian circles, that it is incompatible with being born again to have moods of depression/melancholy, that we should always be filled with the joy of the Lord.

"I think a Christian can have depression," Edith commented, "if only due to metabolism imbalance. Depression generated by such a cause cannot be shaken instantly."

What happens when joy *doesn't* come?

"Then people begin to wonder what unconfessed sin has come between them and God? They begin to doubt their salvation in many instances."

She wrote in *What Is a Family?*: "Everyone who has a long series of illnesses, a handicapping illness, a tragic accident, or a great disappointment in some physical area should consider the truth that the devil would like to make us feel rebellious against God, cry out against Him, say something like, 'Why should this happen to me!' "

But when we are downcast, ironically, is often when the greatest spiritual victories can be manifested—because we are telling God, 'Lord, I'm Yours regardless of the circumstances, happy or sad, high or low.' If we get into the rut, the trap of wanting fellowship only if it is on our terms, the potential for disaster is enormous.

"For so long we have encountered other people's problems/ tragedies," Edith said, her voice barely above a whisper, "and have helped them, have been God's instruments in changing their lives, have 'extracted' the cancer of atheism, etc., but, now, there is something growing, spreading inside my husband and I am powerless to do anything."

At that point she could only sit back and wait, watch the treatments play havoc with his appetite, his weight, his mental perspective (the bouts of depression, nervousness, etc.).

*   *   *   *   *

"Have you ever thought what difference it would make in your life if you found out, at some future date, that you, too, had cancer as your father does?" I asked Priscilla. "Especially *vis-a-vis* your children?"

"I have no reason to suppose that it won't happen to me," she replied. "There is some talk about cancer being hereditary. But then why shouldn't I be the one in the hijacked plane who is killed, or the one who is run over by an automobile. In other words, let us enjoy this day that God has given us rather than be concerned about tomorrow. We live in an abnormal universe, and a hurt universe, and Christ has asked us to continue on until He comes back again or until we die. We should not be one person when everything is going well, and another when things are collapsing for us."

She paused briefly, then: "I think personal moments of crisis in a family help us to realize how fortunate it is when things are going well and we *can* be joyful. *But this is not the norm.*"

"When your father's condition became apparent, did you have any problem with the denial symptoms? Did you try to convince yourself that it wasn't true or, failing that, did you say that he would 'get over it' quickly enough?"

"Not really. You know, I do expect *something* to happen all the time. It's not that I'm a pessimistic person, but I think that that's the way the world is. Ignoring this, trying to smother it in emotional frenzy is a retreat from reality and from *truth*. I doubt God wants us to deceive ourselves. You see, I am so surrounded by those with such sad stories that you come to realize what our lot is in life."

"One of the most persuasive arguments in favor of family life, it would seem, is the mutual support the members can give one another. Isn't that true?"

"Definitely. Mom's a great support to Daddy, for example. She's very brave. Nevertheless I'm sure it took a lot out of her, but we've been there as *her* support. She's had so much to do: seeing that he gets the right diet; seeing that he is comfortable; all the other aspects that she has had to handle. She's simply exhausted. I mean, she throws herself always into any battle, doing her best for everyone."

Familiar touches helped to transform the apartment they lived in for those months in the United States: floral arrangements; photos; etc. The surroundings carried with them links with *L'Abri*. When you are in the midst of a nightmare, not knowing the outcome, factors such as this help a bit.

The outcome?

Remission.

"All gone apparently," Priscilla said. "I mean, he's in total remission now. The growth in his stomach—once the size of a baseball—doesn't exist. It's just shrunk into nothingness—not an affected gland, nothing in his bone marrow. For the rest of his life there'll have to be regular blood tests to monitor his condition, but, right now, well, we're rejoicing."

*   *   *   *   *

It was getting chilly. Edith and I were standing on a quiet mountainside near their home.

The air was slightly misty, but refreshing. Life was good here. Yes, there were severe pressures from time to time, but God had blessed in ways that none of them could have dreamed of many years ago when they left the United States for Switzerland. They had touched hundreds, perhaps thousands, of lives since their first chalet had been purchased. Those who came found that the Schaeffers truly did *care* about them, truly did want to help in any way possible.

We talked about a great deal—how modern life seemed calculated to bring about despair; the discomforting trends in the evangelical world; important matters affecting the body of Christ in its manifold parts.

At that time the prospect of cancer wasn't even hinted, let alone a reality.

"We're ready for whatever the Lord wants to bring to our lives," Edith was saying. "We've experienced so much through others that we're prepared for anything."

Then we walked back to the house.

Nellie Connally

(Note: This chapter is in three parts: Nellie Connally's interview; with additional insight by Katie Brill, who is Nellie's mother; as well as the Connally's son, John III. We felt it crucial to show how faith and love have been integral aspects of life in this family over three generations.)

"We are very proud of our children," Nellie was saying, "because they have matured as human beings very well in terms of their ability to face life. It's difficult, I think, for children to grow up having public parents. Avoiding emotional problems is a miracle. We've been very successful indeed, even though a daughter died tragically years ago. We felt her loss very deeply, of course, but eventually we came to live with it. Yes, despite this, we have been blessed." ·

The key is that Nellie and John were *aware* of the problems that could have developed. They planned to create as "normal" an atmosphere as possible under the circumstances when John was elected Governor of Texas and their lives changed so drastically.

"We all lived together at the governor's mansion," Nellie continued. "We were together a great deal of the time; the capitol building was right across the street. We had a pretty good family unit in those days, tight and warm and loving."

But—as I was to discover about Nellie again and again during the interview—this remarkable woman is given· to real candor. You get the impression she doesn't know the meaning of deceit. Hence, she admitted that being a P.K., Public Kid, has many of the same pressures as being another kind of P.K., Pastor's Kid.

"Oh, it is hard on them," she stated, "very hard on children whose parents are in the public eye. Though they were invited to many different affairs, neither John or I insisted that they go along when they really didn't want to do so. We would say to them, 'You have been invited to go to this with us and you can if you want to go.' Sometimes they would go and sometimes they would not. It is terribly wrong to force children to do things that have little influence on the important aspects of their lives. Going to a party or not should be up to them. Getting them to decide is part of equipping them for making decisions later on when they are on their own. Of course, the larger moral, spiritual issues require a firmer hand. But so many parents dominate everything their children do."

What has been the result? Are their youngsters self-sufficient today, happy, well-adjusted?

"Definitely! They are very super young people who have learned to roll with the punches. And, you know, life's full of punches. We've had a lot of hard knocks. Yet they've come through very well."

Like that day in November a decade and a half ago.

"John was spared for a reason," she said, grimacing a little. "Otherwise he really should have been killed. Yet God allowed him to live. The reason may not be the presidency but then there's another. It was so close. We all could have died that day."

"Where was he shot?" I asked.

"Through the shoulder. The bullet came out under his nipple. It crushed his wrist and went into his knee. He had been in the process of turning when the shot was fired."

"How seriously was he hurt?"

"Badly. If I hadn't pulled him down into my lap, well—you know, it all happened so quickly. Yet, in an instant, I knew what to do. I was just trying to get him out of the line of fire, so they wouldn't hurt him anymore.

"By pulling him over into my lap, his own arm closed the wound. It was the kind you get on the battlefield. You can strangle to death on your own breathing. In war bandages or whatever are stuffed into it to close it."

She paused, then: "For a long time I would awaken at night to have it just replay itself in my mind. But I learned that you compound the nightmare by having it continue to haunt you. You must push it back—never to be forgotten but not allowed to dominate you."

"How long did John have to recuperate?"

"Several weeks. Then we went back to Austin and he developed a blood clot, and he had to go into the hospital there for awhile. But he slowly and carefully recovered. For a time he couldn't write with his right hand, so he had to do the best he could with his left hand. Even while he was at Parkland Hospital in Dallas, the business of being a governor had to continue. So they moved his 'office' in there."

"What part did prayer play during that period?" I asked.

"Considerable. It was a constant communion with Him. We didn't vocalize it often. We just sat and prayed to ourselves, and we knew others were praying, too."

Over the years I've interviewed hundreds of people whose lives are subjected to the glare of the public spotlight: actors, actresses, senators, governors, and so on. The impact is virtually the same in all instances. The public demands a great deal. Not all are able to endure the pressures as ably as have the Connallys.

"The lack of privacy certainly is difficult," Nellie admitted. "The demands on John that force him to be on the road so much also aren't very pleasant. But we decided a long time ago that being in a fishbowl just meant having to adjust to the circumstances; if we didn't want the bad points, we'd have to give up the good ones as well. There are negative and positive aspects in any way of life, any profession. We are totally committed to what we are doing.

"Both of us enjoy people very much. I enjoy being with them, and I can talk forever. I am never at a loss as to what to say. All of this holds true when the encounters are on a one-to-one basis or with small groups. But something terrible happens if I have to stand in front of a microphone before an audience."

124

It was obvious how much Nellie loved John. Their closeness came out a number of times during our conversation:

"We wives learn to tolerate the bad times and to love the good. You can see in your fella when he's in pain and when he's joyous; when things are going well, and when they're going bad. We just kind of learn what to do about it. John is a very compassionate man, and he really projects way into the future—a strange kind of political person, one most people aren't used to seeing. As a rule, most politicians are interested in the next election, and only in the next election. John couldn't care less. He wants only to do the best that he can. When he does that, and he thinks he's done all he can do, then he wants to go on and tackle something else. If you disagree with him, he's sorry, but he has to project his thinking for this country in the direction he thinks is right."

It is said that every decent man starts out similarly in politics and then is corrupted by compromise and a great deal else. Values are trampled upon—and in time decency is forgotten.

"But you don't have to fall into that quicksand . . . unless all you are interested in is the next election. If you're ultimately interested only in yourself, then morality and decency are just day-to-day. Then, too, whatever happens in terms of John's ambitions, we're not going to dissolve. As long as John is able he's going to be doing helpful things, whatever his political office happens to be. He wants the United States to be a good country for future generations."

John Connally is far from being a perfect individual.

"He has a temper," Nellie admitted, "but he knows how to curb it, and he doesn't really explode. He's been a firm father. I would say that the children felt his hand as they were growing up. Which is probably why they turned out so well; they were disciplined when this was necessary.

"Then, too, they realized how important we felt Christ should be in their lives. They went to Sunday school and church services, even when John and I weren't able to do so.

"We gave the children their little Bibles just as soon as they started going to Sunday school. We have one up in our guestroom for whoever might spend the night there. Being a Christian shows up in the big things and in these little ways, too."

Unlike the Carter family, the Connallys haven't been exceedingly vocal about their Christianity.

"That's true," Nellie agreed. "But we're still devoted Chris-

125

tians, worshiping in church—though not as much as my mother would like, as I'm sure she'll tell you—and saying our prayers every night. I often ask the Lord to help me be a good wife and a good mother, and in so doing I know I'll be more pleasing to Him because that's what He's wanted me to be from the very start."

Phoniness irritates Nellie Connally.

"Oh, it's just awful in people. I try to be honest and straightforward all the time. Deception is a terrible evil, in my opinion. And when it's carried on at a high governmental level, well, the consequences are unfortunate.

"I learned a long time ago that you may not be the most intellectual person in the world, and you may not have all the answers to everything, but if you will be very honest about what you do think then you're going to get along better in this world than if you try to be something you're not, or pretend to know something you don't know."

The disintegration of the family unit concerns her very much.

"It's a real danger," she said. "I tried always to teach my children the love of family and home and God. I taught them to have manners, to say, 'Yes, sir,' or 'No, sir,' or 'Yes, ma'am,' or 'No, ma'am.' Little family unit things that are basic in life.

"Even so, I think our children grow totally as human beings only when they become parents themselves. Then they realize how right *their* parents were in so many things; and where their parents were wrong. They can set about correcting these areas with *their* children. I think you have to be a mother before you can relate fully to the role your parents had as heads of the household.

"When I was a child, we had a happy, fun, pleasant home life. We didn't have unnecessary things; but we certainly had enough to eat, and plenty to wear, and we vacationed. There was excess of nothing, as the expression goes, but we enjoyed ourselves. Our vacation was not a cruise or a ski trip. We went fishing or camping or both, and we went as a family. We kept active. And, you know, my mother, God bless her, is still active today. She gets up at 4:30 each weekday morning and goes to a hospital nearby to work with cancer patients. This means a lot to her since my father died of cancer years ago.

"My children call her the last of the red hot mamas. There's more of a generation gap between my mother and me than there is between my mother and her grandchildren. They adore her. She's a real lady."

126

"Well, I'll tell you about Nellie," remarked Katie Brill, her mother, as we sat in her apartment. "My children started going to Sunday school when they were little bitsy folk, even in the cradle room. I think when someone is brought up in this environment, and they live this way, well, it's difficult to tell when they became born again. Being born again doesn't have to involve a spectacular moment of conversion. With Nellie it came in stages, over the years. But, yes, she is indeed a wonderful Christian."

"But she doesn't talk about it in quite so outspoken a way as, say, Rosalyn Carter would. Why do you think that is the case?"

"Because it was made into a political thing—and Nellie feels that making your relationship with Christ a matter of politics is wrong. She'll always be more subdued for that reason. I know, for certain, that she has accepted Christ into her life as Savior and Lord.

"It has amazed me, in recent days, how many people are born again and don't realize that their lives fit that label. Why, in my Sunday-school class, I have people ask me from time to time what being born again means. After I explain it to them, they say, 'Well, I certainly am.' "

"Is John really a solid Christian?" I asked.

"Yes. And he's wonderful. You know mothers-in-law are never prejudiced. Anyway, he's one of the most wonderful men I've ever known. John believes that there's some good in everybody. As he once said, 'What we need to do is reach way down in the barrel and find that good and build on it. Don't put your feet on their head and push them down.'

"I remember when he was Secretary of the Navy, and he was reading the minutes from his predecessor. He saw where there had been prayer. He asked those present, 'Why did you all stop the prayer?' He was told, 'Well, we don't have a chaplain now.' He replied, 'Well, we're going to have our first meeting together today and, while we don't have a chaplain, we'll still have prayer.' So John had prayer. One of the fellows there called Nellie to tell her about it. I think that's pretty nice.

"When he was a little boy, his mother was talking to him one day and said, 'What would you like to be when you are older?' He said, 'I'd like to be a cowboy.' So she said, 'Well, you can be a cowboy all right, maybe for awhile, son, but what about later, after you graduate from college?' He told her, 'Oh, I guess a lawyer.'

She asked, 'If not that, then what?' He said, 'I guess I'll be a preacher.' His mother recalled, later, that when he was eight he was in the saddle; and after he finished college, he was a lawyer. And she said, 'Who knows, someday he may just do a little preaching.' "

*   *   *   *   *

"I just feel that there's so much of Christ in this family," I was saying. "Even when it's not discussed out in the open you can honestly feel the Lord is here."

"Faith's a family matter with us," John Connally III told me before dinner at his home. "We all went to church, and prayed often, and together. When we were in college, my wife and I involved ourselves with Campus Crusade. We had meetings in my fraternity house and in her sorority house, where we met with representatives of Campus Crusade. After we got married, and I graduated from law school, and moved to Houston, we started looking around for a church home. We found River Oaks Baptist Church. It is really a very small country-type church, family-oriented, low-key.

"We have a lot of activities in the church, at different times of the year. This seems only natural to my wife and me. It's the way we both were raised by our respective parents.

"I don't feel that we ever become *complete* Christians. You grow in Christ throughout your life, and I think we are continuing to do so. It's real, this growth, not artificial. Also, it's just the sort of thing, our Christian life, that we feel doesn't require publicity. It's not something you hide, but it's not something you boast about, either, because then it seems self-serving."

"What is Christianity?" I asked.

"Christianity is the form; and Christ is the person," John replied. "You become a Christian by accepting Christ totally into your life. You can't accept Him as an historical figure only; as a great teacher only. You must accept Him as Son of God come to die for our sins.

"I'm not a tremendous witness for Him. There are times when I should witness that I don't. And there are times when I think about doing so, and I don't. And there are times when I don't even think about it, and I should. I ought to be better, I know.

"But when I do witness, I try to be perceptive as to the person to whom I am witnessing. It very much depends upon the individual, what their situation is. For some people, a certain type of witnessing would turn them off. You have to do it differently each time, I think. In one instance you would perhaps suggest that the two of you should pray together. In another instance, you would take a much more businesslike approach. I had a lawyer friend once who was concerned, because he was atheistic, about his child going to a school that had religious teaching involved. I couldn't get out the Bible and start reading. So the way I tried to relate was to say, 'Well, look, you don't have a problem with your child being exposed at an early age to football, baseball, basketball, other sports and other interests, even though you know that when he's a senior in high school he may discard baseball and never play it again. But you'd like to see him exposed to hunting and fishing and all those other things so that later on he'll have some background to make a choice.' And he said, 'Well, sure.' I said, 'What's the difference? Why shouldn't he have the opportunity to make a choice himself?' And I invariably find that such men have no real retort. When they are confronted by common sense, by truth, they are usually silenced."

*   *   *   *   *

"Our children turned out so well," Nellie told me. "But John and I are terribly concerned about others. As I said earlier, the shaking apart of the family unit has accelerated over the years. During the sixties, and more recently, there's been a new program coming out for every conceivable need, promising a great deal but giving very little in return. Young people are growing up distrustful of government—and they are raising their youngsters the same way.

"John sensed this when he was Governor of Texas. He would call and tell the President, 'Please, no more programs. We just can't handle all these programs.' This would really upset my husband, and he finally got to where his calls would be ignored.

"Take ERA, for example. I've always been in favor of equal rights for anybody who should have them. When I was in high school, I wrote a paper entitled, 'Equal Educational Opportunities for Blacks and Whites.' Now that was eons ago. I still believe that everybody should have equal educational and other opportunities. But I think also that these should be on the basis of your qualifications, your ability, not because you're a woman, not because you're black, not because you're white, not because you're anything like this. Rather, because you are qualified. I don't think qualified people, ultimately, need any kind of group to push them on, to march for them, or to make demands for them.

"So we had too much chaos in years gone by. You could hardly expect the young generation to take it all in stride. We just had too much permissiveness and families started to split apart. We need to get back to basic values, to hold on to those that are still left. Things will get worse before they're any better. We've got a fight on our hands, a fight for a return to morality, to ethics, to decency. I don't know if any one man has the answer. But all men of conscience should try their best, else they risk seeing this great country go down the drain."

Nellie feels that strong families and religious faith go hand in hand.

"Faith has taken a back seat along with the family as people push toward more and more materialism, looking to government to solve their problems, and then acting with bitterness when government doesn't.

"There is a general lack of restraint, of discipline, in life today. That's especially true in the family. I think this is terribly, terribly wrong. If parents don't care, if they let their children get away with anything, then we can't condemn the younger generation for its excesses."

Gloria Hope Hawley

What is a normal life? That is a question with an answer that varies from culture to culture. A child growing up in Wheaton, Illinois, would have a normalcy that would be the antithesis of a child in Calcutta, India or Moscow or Lima, Peru.

Even within the cultural differences there is an underlying thread that draws every child everywhere together. Can he hear? Can he speak? Can he see? Can he walk?

For the retarded child in any country, the answer to such questions is usually yes, to a greater or lesser degree. Admittedly the more extreme forms of retardation change the situation substantially. But, generally speaking, the retarded child *can* hear, *can* speak (after a fashion), *can* see, *can* walk.

Yet doing all this, which every normal child can do, the retarded boy and girl falls short in one overriding area. He can't put it all together. His mind is incapable of sorting out the pieces in his world and making life work in a coherent fashion. From time to time there are flashes, moments when he nearly understands, when he comes so close to breaking out of that "strange" little world in which he finds himself, a world with a wall around it that separates him from *another* world. But they are only flashes, fading as rapidly as they indistinctly appear, the makeup of his brain unable to lock onto them and expand them, grasp what they mean, what they *are*. It's like a TV or radio set that is just a little, just a little, "off the channel."

While he is *here*, the product of a union between his mother and his father, and while he eats and sleeps and lives and breathes, he'll never be an integral part of the adult world—*not as long as he lives.*

Gloria Hope Hawley has been through all of this, and much more. Only the mother of a retarded child or children can understand. Those who have not had the traumas cannot perceive the pain.

"Some people, looking at your situation, would say, 'Tsk, tsk, what a shame,' " I said as I interviewed Gloria at the Hawley residence in Fullerton, California. "How do you react to this kind of mind-set?"

"Yeah, it is a shame, Roger," she replied. "On more than a surface level that's just what it is. But, usually, I hear them call it a tragedy. A terrible, awful, rotten tragedy."

She paused, then: "Now I looked up tragedy in the dictionary before I wrote my book, *Laura's Psalm*. My life, the lives of my children, none of *that* is a tragedy because the main characters triumph; they don't go down the tube.

"You know, I really like it if people approach me in the negative, a clear-cut negative—because it gives me a marvelous opportunity to say, 'May I explain the difference between tragedy and triumph?' The difference is the indwelling Holy Spirit."

It's a warm day. She feels the bright sun on her face. She raises up one hand to touch her skin, as though puzzled by the warmth. What is that lovely feeling?

She looks upward, sensing that it has come from above. But there is a brightness, and it hurts her eyes, and she pulls away.

And, suddenly, not even she knowing why, a tear forms on her cheek. . . .

Gloria wants to reach the maximum number of people when she writes or speaks before a group or does a TV show.

"I'm beginning to feel the pressure myself," Gloria continued. "Time is so precious, what with my obligations with Laura and

Craig. I would like to reach the most people in the least amount of time. I prepare for and pray about twenty as much as I do for two thousand, because in all instances they get the full thrust of Christ in me."

I hesitated for a moment, thinking of all that Gloria was telling me, thinking of Laura and Craig. Their physical bodies were, respectively, twenty-one years and fourteen years of age, but their mental ages were only three and seven.

"How rough was it before Christ came into your life eight years ago?" I asked.

"Horrible. *That* was a tragedy. Our home was not a sanctuary. I had all my priorities backwards. I was so very anxious about my children. I wanted to control their complete environment. I was making them hothouse plants.

"I just wanted to surround them. I loved them fiercely, fiercely, which made me very combative. But I did everything with hostility.

"I listened to advice that didn't make me feel any different: (1) Put Laura away; (2) Medicate, medicate, medicate. It was always the same. I never medicated those kids, except with anticonvulsive agents. I was never a mood or attitude changer . . . praise God. Today the pendulum is swinging the other way; we just don't do that sort of thing anymore.

"The net effect upon me was corrosive fear, anxiety, hostility toward everyone—primarily toward God. My responses were typical of an immature person, someone who focused on people and things."

Then it changed. Bit by bit, moment by moment, growing in Christ became a reality. But it didn't mean that there weren't problems along the way. There continue to be many of these even now.

He was looking at television. The images interested, then puzzled him. He couldn't quite understand what was going on. But a moment or two really caught his attention.

Then his mind started to wander. He was thinking of a meadow where he had romped with his mother, his father, his sister. It was great there, pretty flowers and butterflies that flew up before him as he came upon them. He could hear sounds, strange yet wonderful; and the wind touched his face gently . . .

"Laura was first, of course," Gloria continued, "and then Craig. Craig was greatly looked for and longed for and planned for. We thought that he would not be as Laura was. We were so happy with the prospect. We went through all the blood tests, the rest of it, and there was nothing, absolutely nothing that made us uneasy. Everything pointed to the fact that we were not to have another retarded child.

"At the beginning Craig seemed perfect . . . until he couldn't sit up. He was still alert, still grasping, but he couldn't sit up. That was the beginning. We discovered he had hydrocephalus, which is water on the brain. By the time we got him to a surgeon, it had stopped, however, and didn't threaten his life. You just don't open a skull for any old reason, you know, and there was no operation."

Laura's handicap really is severe. She suffers, on top of everything else, from echolalia, which is a mimicking condition. Unable to form a sentence of her own, unable to initiate a thought of any depth, she falls back on the trap of repeating what she hears, and even then only the simplest of words, phrases. Say "Hello" to Laura and you will hear that word again and again from her. She seems so fragile when she says it, a little like a bird that is groping to imitate something its owner has said. Even this venture, so tentative, into a world of "normal" communication, is embarked upon with hesitancy. The expression on her face gives an observer the impression that Laura is scared, that she is "speaking" but doesn't know quite what that means or what she is doing. You could put a baby in the middle of a huge shopping mall and get the same puzzled response.

"Is there any kind of job that either could take care of?" I asked.

"Craig may but you can be fooled so easily about the overall picture in each case. These children develop splinter skills. They don't move ahead on an even basis, but rather they develop like a flame, a little bit here, a little bit there. Laura has very good basic common sense, but she's very afraid of making a mistake so her movements are slow. She doesn't say a great deal because she's afraid of rejection. She has suffered at the hands of other children, their cruelty, their lack of sensitivity and understanding about her condition."

"Do they perceive sorrow as deeply as we do? One of the cliches of society is that they are in their happy little world and maybe it's a blessing for them after all."

"That makes society feel a lot better, doesn't it?"

Gloria smiles a bit, memories flooding in on her.

"Laura has deep currents that I can't reach. She starts weeping. I don't know why and I can't reach her. I don't know what's hurting her inside."

Sitting there, surrounded by those who love her, it's like a tall concrete fence. Communication is blocked. She may be lonely. She may be in pain. A normal child would say, "Mom, I have a pain in my stomach." But Laura can't do that. It may be that, over the years, facing the inability to express herself, she has partially given up even the attempt. So she suffers alone, isolated, just her and the pain or the sorrow or whatever.

"Does Laura understand the concept of God?"

"She understands in her soul better than I do. She isn't hindered by a lot of ego or selfish things or materialism. Listen, Jesus talked about having the heart of a child. Well, Laura and Craig will be children for as long as they live.

"My youngsters teach me so much about dependence upon the Father. I see parallels all the time. They are living out so much of what Jesus said about being as a little child."

Gloria paused, then went on: "I think, to a degree, all of us are retarded children. Everyone is handicapped to a certain extent because none of us is perfect. That's why God sent the Rehabilitator to fix what's wrong with us.

"Craig will come to me and say, 'Mom, I'm dirty. Mom, I'm dirty.' And I'll respond, 'Craig, I hate that, I hate that. Don't be dirty. Don't do that in your pants.' I clean him up and he weeps, 'I'm sorry. I'm sorry, Mom. I love you.' You know what I'll usually tell him: 'I love you, too, my son.' I won't hold back from him. He mustn't feel rejected in any way.

"Then I think to myself, 'Lord, I'm filthy. I stink. I did that again. But I love You, Lord.' And I know that He continues to love me, no matter what I do. He has said to me, through His Word, 'Yes, I love you, my child. Let me clean you with the blood of Jesus Christ.' There is a parallel, you know. We are all retarded children in His sight—yet some of us won't accept rehabilitation."

Once, when I called Gloria on the phone, Laura was having difficulty.

"When Laura became ill, I was beset with some of the same old anxieties. I was amazed at myself. How little I had learned. I was back at square one. I hurt. I couldn't control my responses of anxiety for my child, and this distorted my priorities again. You

135

see, I had to let head knowledge be forged into heart knowledge by the Lord.

"I was awakened in the middle of the night to find Laura drawn back in a bow, with her head almost touching her heels, her fists clenched, and this death grin on her face, turning blue. This was our introduction to the new episode in her life.

"It's a progressive brain disease, complicated probably by adhesions due to scarring. But we just don't want to dissect her to see what or why, because that would be very hard for her.

"Each time I thought she was dying, because she didn't breathe for so long. They were very bad seizures, a symptom of something working on her that none of us could be aware of. Then when we started giving her anticonvulsive medicine, it turned out the proportion needed to subdue her was toxic. So here I had this child who was weeping, vomiting, and convulsing, but I couldn't give her enough of the one medication which could have helped her.

"I walked a tightrope all summer, trying to give her enough medication to subdue her racking seizures and also trying to maintain her physiology. My daughter who is a comfortable, easy, pleasant, basically happy child became enraged, negative, wept. She spent whole days just weeping. Oh, it was devastating, just devastating, because I hurt for her and I couldn't make her better."

But there is quite another factor in being the parents of retarded children, one that Gloria and her husband Chan know all too well.

The expense.

"The medical and legal necessities are awful. Craig's teeth are in bad shape; he needs a whole orthodontist's job. Laura has crooked teeth, too, but hers are that way because she doesn't use her muscles properly. If we straighten the teeth, she'll just push them back out again.

"But such costs are only part of the picture. The legalities one encounters as a retarded child approaches the age of eighteen are horrendous. At that age you are no longer considered the parents but, rather, the *guardians*. We've had to employ the services of a lawyer, go to court twice, and, also, get Laura her own legal counsel.

"I believe the laws governing this were drafted as a protective measure by someone who did not live with the problem. They thought that if we didn't measure up to an outsider's exact determination of what we should be, we could lose our children. Well, when society begins to take charge in such a manner, judging which child will stay with a family, and which will be taken away, or who will live and who will die, as in the case of abortion, we have then begun the first steps that Germany took years ago, ridding ourselves of the unproductive person.

"This is the trend, though. Pulling the plug. There are so many, many ramifications. The lawyer who represented Laura was a no-nonsense, no-jokes-please type. At one point he said to me, 'I have just come from the home of a sixty-year-old woman. Her son was in his forties. She has kept him home all these years, because he was retarded. She did not avail herself of the current public resources for that man, and I had him removed.' Just like that—taken away from his home, with no comprehension on *his* part as to what was going on. In effect, he had no choice in the matter."

. . . *no choice.*

The antithesis of democracy. The state has control. The state can interfere under any pretext, and all of it under the guise of protecting an individual's civil rights.

"Is sex a problem with the retarded?" I asked.

"Well, of course, they do have sexual feelings. They're human beings in every sense of the word, but simply more limited than others. Their hormones are operative, yet they are totally innocent as far as sex is concerned.

"I am a very protective mother. The current professional opinion is that they should be encouraged in terms of sex, and even allowed to masturbate to completion, to climax. Laura, as a young adult woman, should be on some contraceptive pill, and allowed to engage in sexual experimentation. If it feels good to her, I am told, let her do it, because that is her right as a human being.

"Let me tell you and everyone who reads this that I, as a Christian mother, don't want either Laura or Craig awakened, because it will not be to fulfillment as God describes it in Genesis. Why dangle an impossibility in front of them, just for physical gratification? I am certain that I open myself up for criticism by taking this stance, but that is the way it is in this house.

"The children are functioning perfectly as God designed them. We are appreciating the gifts because we've read the manual, and we're operating under the owner's warranty. They belong to God, and God doesn't make mistakes."

Evelyn Christenson

Evelyn, so many Christians fear death. What do you think about this?

I personally have no suicidal tendencies, but I'm sure looking forward to the day when I'll be with the Lord—that fantastic day. I get very excited about it. I really do. I think it's ridiculous for any Christian to fear dying. They should be looking for Jesus.

Our whole culture cooperates with this fear. We try to put people on drugs so they won't know they're dying. Death is treated as the great *permanent* separation.

My husband and I have an agreement that we are going to have the dignity of dying. The dignity of dying is as God wants us to die. That's how we want to approach this important adventure.

No matter how painful?

I'm not going to say that. There will obviously be painkillers. We're just not in favor of keeping each other alive on life-sustaining equipment until way past the point at which God is calling us. Our materialistic society assumes that this life is all we have, and that life sustainment is a blessing, delaying the inevitable slide into oblivion.

Like that day her brother died. Evelyn's mother wasn't prepared. It came so suddenly. And then they had to go to the mortuary to make arrangements.

"I can't," the older woman said.

"But it's necessary, Mother, it's part of life," Evelyn replied. "He's with our Lord."

"I know but—"

Evelyn took her frail little mother in her arms and said, "This is the ultimate, dear one. Romans 8:28 promises that *all* things work together for good because we know and love Him. Please, please remember that."

Over the years Evelyn's father had died, and her little daughter Judy who was only seven months old. Yet she soon found the peace that passes all understanding, slicing through denial into acceptance.

There is an awful lot of potential for disaster when children are being raised. How can one ever honestly encourage a married couple to have children?

Children are a heritage from the Lord. Sure, it's hard. Sure, there are risks, and the price is high. But the rewards so over shadow the price that there is no contest in my opinion. I don't know what I would do at this point if my children were all grown and gone. I'd miss them severely. Sure we cry a lot, but there are also tears of joy because we have one another.

Aren't there risks in all worthwhile areas of life? If I'm going to do something great for God, there are risks. Sometimes we can gain through losing. We can strengthen our personalities, our moral stamina. I have a banker friend who said, "You know, unless you're willing to risk losing money, you're not going to make any real gains in this financial world." The principle applies in so many areas of our existence.

What are the rewards, really?

The joy and the love. The sharing. Even the moments of "crisis," because these can change us for the better if we allow them. If we *do* change, that's a reward also.

139

I remember when my first child turned 18 years of age. She was a very independent one. She'd just finished med school at the University of Minnesota and was a very independent thinker. Suddenly, she told me she never wanted to hear her mother's philosophy of life again—that she had had enough.

Well, I went "underground" for fourteen months. During that time I stayed in God's Word. I wanted to be the mother God wanted me to be, to learn even from such a harsh experience.

What I did come to realize was the need of a child to cut the apron strings. Some do it with more grace than did my daughter, but they do it nevertheless. The alternative is the horror of a child who doesn't ever cut them. This is a very bad thing.

I bled emotionally when my daughter did what she did. I almost bled to death in fact. But I realized the utter necessity of hanging on, loving her, praying for her, keeping an open door. It's amazing how fast youngsters really do start to come back. They have to find themselves. They have to become individuals. The saddest thing in the world is a grown body still hanging on to mother, and mother spoon-feeding that child.

When they find out who they are, then they can come back as your friend. My children are my friends.

We all must give account of ourselves, someday, before God. Not through our parents, either.

Disastrous things can happen when God's plan for individuals is thwarted. When human possessiveness takes over. When—

Such as the teenage girl who was given a rifle for Christmas, and used that rifle to kill three other human beings. Why did she do it? For kicks. To break the monotony of a dull day.

Then there are the boys buried under their murderer's house. Boys who were enticed by him, then abused, then slaughtered. Perhaps they, too, wanted to break away, to be independent, to—

Or the sniper who shot a dozen or more people. Or the—

We may never know, really, really know, what went wrong. What influence was improper. What divine rule was not followed. But the fact remains that, adult or not, these killers or victims had childhoods which made them what they were/are. Their parents cared too much or too little. To be independent they had to kill others or engage in the tasting of forbidden fruit.

You can have cases where bad homes turn out "monsters." But what about great people who also come from bad homes? How do you explain these?

They refused to allow themselves to be limited by their backgrounds. God will involve us in a changing process all our lives if we but allow Him to do so. We have this tremendous potential within us.

God can take us out of bad environments and make of us what He will if *we* don't stand in the way. He sees the potential of each individual. Even if parents are rotten, God uses other influences. Maybe a Sunday-school teacher or a friend or someone else. Some of the greatest Christian leaders did not have the most solid of childhoods.

Let's think about the girl who was so completely unloved, hated, and rejected as a child; yet who is spending her life with children, young people, showing them the love of Jesus. This leads her into an understanding and a forgiveness, and a fulfillment.

Parents should be careful to be affectionate. Denial of affection can be so devastating. Touching a child is important—touching and holding and squeezing and telling our children that we love them. If there's enough of the right kind of love in a home, it can float over everything. It can conquer anything.

There has been an attitude about in the land that a boy or a girl who requires an awful lot of this hugging, kissing, touching approach is essentially an emotionally weak child. But I think that that's an old Victorian attitude that keeps hanging on and is really dangerous. Jesus did a lot of touching. He himself wept. The idea that men especially shouldn't cry is ridiculous. I think it may be a sign of weakness if they don't cry or don't touch.

The view that men can handle everything, that they should pick themselves up by the bootstraps, isn't a Christian view. If they can do all of this, then they don't really need God.

Not too long ago, on television, I saw a relatively young woman being interviewed. She'd had, over the years, two children without benefit of matrimony. She said that she didn't even come close to being engaged. 'Oh, I could have had an abortion,' she said, 'but I simply decided to have my children.' She said this in such a way as to seem terribly noble. What do you think about this? A girl has an affair or even a one-night stand with some guy. She becomes pregnant, and she decides to forego an abortion.

141

Instead she wants the child to stay with her. What do you think about this whole syndrome? Is she to be admired? Or what?

It's a situation being repeated in our country virtually every day. Such a girl is probably not a Christian. I can't conceive that she would be. It's a big, deep thing, Roger, and it's between the girl and God. Parents can't really do much about this. It's what the girl decides. I do have to say that I admire her for not having an abortion, though I despise the life-style that made her twice a mother without being married. I admire her up to a point for keeping those children. But I think they would have been much better off had they gone into a home where they could get love from two parents.

There are many, many fine homes today where people are just crying for children. She is depriving the children of a lot of things by seeing to it that they're not put into such a home. Then, later on in life, she's likely to face youngsters who are a real misery to her.

We look at the girl who killed three human beings and our tendency is toward derision. "What a monster!" we might exclaim. "What a terrible sin she has committed."

And terrible it is to take the life of another human being. To say, without any apparent remorse, "It was a dull day. I needed some kicks."

But what made her like she is? How insensitive were her parents? She probably reached the age that she did without having Christ in her life. While now she seems unconcerned, almost wallowing in the publicity, the "glory" of it all, what happens later, in the quietness, the isolation of her prison cell when, in a moment of clarity, she knows, she knows, she knows what she has done?

Virginia Womach

Don't let that creature be my husband!!

Her mind screamed those words a dozen times in rapid succession. What she was looking at was a mummy from some horror film. Merrill had been so handsome. Surely this—

It was a nightmare to which she would have to grow accustomed but one that the Lord gave her amazing strength to endure. Yet, having said that, *nothing* could completely obviate the awfulness of what she was called upon to do.

"Pulling the scabs off to let the poison ooze out was the most difficult task I had ever had to do in my life," Virginia Womach said as we talked in their condominium overlooking Waikiki. "It was horrible. The nurse showed me how. It had to be done several times daily. First his face, then his hands. It took so long that the nurse would work on one side and I would work on the other to save some time. This all was training for me when Merrill came home. I didn't relish doing it each time, because of not wanting to hurt him.

"I had no way of knowing how he felt. He was totally conscious each time. A burn heals in an entirely different way from a regular wound. A burn heals from the outside in. Ordinary wounds heal from the inside out. So you have to keep picking these scabs off, and keep them off in order for healing to take place inside. Otherwise, under the scab, there'd be a lot more pus and other poisons building up."

"A melodramatic scene in a movie involving a paraplegic might have him confronting his wife at some point and saying, 'I'm useless. I'm hopeless. I'll never be any good for you.' Was there ever such an encounter between you and Merrill?"

"He felt sometimes, when the pain was so great, that he could hardly cope with it. He would ask, 'Why didn't I die in the accident?' Then came the unveiling of his face after the first operation. I nearly fainted because I expected to see a marked improvement. No way. He was worse looking to me than before the operation (because I had gotten used to his looks before the graft). The purpose was to cover up his face because he was hemorrhaging to death; they didn't mold it or shape it to fit the face. They just plain sewed skin on in order to save the man's life.

"I could see the seams. Even after all these years a stitch will work its way to the surface, and he'll have to get a pair of tweezers and pull it out. I have cut stitches and pulled them out many, many times myself."

One of the roughest moments—after the operations, the recuperation—was going out in public for the first time. By and large people were kind, but not always.

"As well-known as he is, Merrill finds that many people just don't know about his story. He'll encounter those who are incredibly insensitive."

Like when a group of teenage boys was standing to one side, watching as he came out of a store, laughing at him. As he walked past, they taunted him even more, calling him tasteless names. It took all of his willpower to restrain himself. He might have had the satisfaction of attacking them, but his hands would have been ripped open in the process, and there was no telling what they might have done to his face. Times like that Merrill would say to himself, "They just don't know any better and they're the ones to be pitied." Then there was the time when Virginia and he were walking down the street.

"Some people were in front of us, coming toward us," she

recalled. "They looked at Merrill, walked around him, ran forward, and then stood and watched him while we walked up to them again. They wanted a second look.

"It was interesting to watch people in a car which had pulled up next to us at a traffic light. They almost went off the road while gawking at Merrill."

At the same time Virginia was so close to Merrill, helping him, watching over him, she felt secure. Someone was depending upon her. She could lose herself in the need of those moments.

"I had always tried to stand *behind* my husband," she told me. "Whatever he wanted to do was okay with me. All the while the inferiority complex that I had faced most of my life was getting worse. Merrill was and still is the mainstay in the family. But all of us needs our own identity. I need to be known for me, too. I have to be known as Virginia. So many people have come up to me and asked a question beginning with, 'Mrs. Merrill?'

"When the children were home, they depended on me. But then when they left, the house seemed so empty. I tried to travel as much as I could with Merrill—but my feet swell to the point where I have to cut the straps off my shoes in order to put them back on. If I sit for any length of time, I retain fluid. So I can't travel well anymore; also changes of climate are especially poor for me."

So, with the children gone, and Merrill traveling such a great deal, Virginia was left to her own devices.

How did it develop, this complex? To anyone not afflicted by it, the impact seems unfathomable. You think of yourself as totally inadequate to most circumstances in life. If people compliment you, or your work, this has hardly any effect because you've so thoroughly discounted your personal worthiness.

"My father and mother were always the ones in my youth that were telling me what to do, when to do it, and how to do it as most parents do. I married at a young age and my husband just picked up from where my parents left off. So I really didn't ever have a time when I, myself, made decisions for myself except when Merrill was on the road. Even here the big decisions would wait until I talked to Merrill on the phone. It seemed like all my life I had had instructions from someone. I didn't really have a chance to think for myself."

Then along came change of life.

"It didn't help my situation, of course," she reflected candidly. "I felt I didn't want to be a pillpusher, and I hoped the Lord would give me the strength to go through this without medication."

"How helpful was Merrill during this?"

"Rather like most men. They don't quite understand the whole thing. So I just had to learn to cope with it, as all women do. I think probably depression set in more than anything. Remember, I was alone so much of the time. All human beings need to be wanted, need to be told that they're loved. And I am one of those particular people who need to be told daily that I'm needed, wanted, and loved."

Having a famous husband, she says, only made matters worse.

"He's sought after by everyone," she said. "People acclaim his talent. But that means I am left in the back pew alone while he's in the limelight, and it gets lonely there, you know."

People would say, 'Where's your husband?' Not how are you? 'Isn't he just wonderful?' And they brushed on by, ready to stand in line just to talk with him for a few seconds.

Merrill's scars are visible. Merrill's ordeal has been the most dramatic one. Virginia is youthful looking, attractive, her skin remarkably unwrinkled. She has it made, they say. Money, cars, a big family, a famous huband.

The difference is that Virginia's scars are not visible, but she has them. They are scars of the emotions.

"I feel my husband's a walking miracle. I really do. I feel that the man, even though he's gone through the accident, and his face is scarred, is beautiful. He's a beautiful man. And I say this from my heart, because the beauty doesn't have to be evident in the skin on the outside. That's what so many people see and judge by. But it's the beauty that we can find inside the person that really counts. You look beyond the physical."

Merrill is a perfectionist. He expects the best from those around him.

"Virginia," I asked next, "do you ever get the impression that you personally have not measured up to his standards?"

"Oh, definitely. I feel that all the time. It's only during the last year and a half that I've been able to pull myself even superficially away from that tendency. Over the years he has grown and matured, whereas I have grown and matured comparatively little."

She felt that she had let him down severely when it turned out that she couldn't give him more than three children.

146

"I had to have a hysterectomy at the age of twenty-seven. I had tumors and these were the type that would have turned cancerous probably. My daughter had to have a hysterectomy at the age of twenty-five because of the same problem."

"Was this propensity inherited?"

"Oh, yes. It's called endometriosis. It's handed down through the mother to the daughter. It cannot be passed through the male, only through the female child. It hits only the ovaries and the female organs."

She paused, looking out at the gradually darkening sky, then: "Every time I see a child to this day, I wish I could have had more. I love babies. I think they're precious, but I'm really thankful for what I had. Yet not giving my husband more only fueled my complex. I felt cheated, disappointed. I also felt that I was less of a woman."

In speaking again of Merrill, she said, "There is pain all the time, in one form or another, for one reason or another. When it's a humid day he feels as though his face is puffing up. But he has no way of perspiring. He feels as though he's got a mask on."

Comparisons between Virginia and Merrill are not as ridiculous as might seem to be at first blush. For she, too, has lived behind a mask for many years. The facade is that of a radiant, self-confident, supremely thankful and happy woman. The difference lies in the fact that Merrill's mask doesn't hide an insecure, unhappy, restless human being. But Virginia's does.

What about those other inconveniences just mentioned?

"His mouth can hardly open up. He can't eat what others of us take for granted: corn on the cob, thick sandwiches, even a hot dog—at least in the regular way. He has to squash it down so that it can be pushed into his mouth.

"And he finds it very difficult to get dental work done. He tends to let his teeth just go without. False teeth would no doubt be a virtual impossibility. He can't close his eyes all the way. The lids were burned away, and the replacement skin just doesn't function completely satisfactorily."

"Did you ever slip into the trap of pitying him?"

"No, I don't think so. I was sorry he had to be in such pain. But pity? No way. We both have always felt that God allowed us to go through all this for a reason. Merrill and I felt definitely that we were chosen because we would prove to be strong enough through God to endure it and still praise the Lord for it."

"Yet," I asked hesitantly, "can you talk about strength, knowing that an inferiority complex is really a heightened form of emotional/psychological weakness?"

"I found strength to help Merrill that I never knew I possessed." (And my own mind went back to my hours with Evelyn LeTourneau, to what she said about the Lord not giving strength *until* we needed it!)

"Whenever I've fallen," Virginia continued, "it's been *my* fault, not God's. I'm the one who did it to myself. Whenever I've been weak, and that's been often, it's because I've not *allowed* His strength into my life. Whenever I've not been by His side, that's when there's been trouble."

"And hasn't that been the case with Merrill, too? When he's gone, your feelings have been intensified."

"Yes. . . ."

Virginia's search began a few years ago. She wanted to find herself. She was a woman experiencing in her middle years what most people go through during their teens and/or college period. At first the search was tentative. How *could* she do something? What would Merrill think? The children? Would they say, "You've not had the fulfillment you need with us all these years? We've not given you the satisfaction you've needed?" Where could she turn? It was so very difficult to explain, something so personal that it might remain locked up inside. It might torment her for the rest of her life, if she didn't find, during her search, that elusive self-image that would enable her to face life as a worthwhile, interesting, even desirable human being—desirable as a friend, a mother, a wife.

But Merrill, for one, hasn't shown any resentment, any disappointment. (Nor have the children, for that matter.)

"He's always wanted me to have the feeling that I'm as good as anybody," she remarked. "He's tried to tell me this. 'You mustn't feel inferior, Virginia, because you're not.' But that didn't do any good. Words are useless in my case. My rebirth to find myself had to come from inside."

That's why one step in the process has been getting the condo. She's furnished it herself. The decision to *do* this was hers, independently arrived at, and without regrets.

"It's good for me over here," she said, smiling. "I have constant contact with Merrill by phone every single day. He calls me or I call him. Over here, by and large, I see people who don't know Merrill. I make friends of my own, not those who become friendly because of him. They don't put me in the back pew, so to speak. They come up to me and say, 'Virginia, it's good to see you.' Rather than, 'Hello, Virginia, where's Merrill?'

"Back in Spokane, when Merrill's on the road, I find fellowship terribly awkward. People keep asking where is Merrill. How can I stand to have him on the road so much? 'Oh, Virginia, you're so brave. I couldn't let my husband be away from me as long as your husband is. My husband loves me too much for us to be separated that length of time.' Though they're trying to be good Christians, they're hurting me to the place where they're pushing me out of the church."

But in Hawaii it's Virginia Womach, not Merrill Womach's wife. She is a person who is being welcomed into a certain social realm because of *herself*, not her husband's fame.

"How do the children react?" I asked.

"They're pleased with the fact that I am trying to be myself. It's what I emphasized in their lives as they were growing up. They encourage me to find my identity. I've taken up oil painting because I feel I can find me in that oil paint. That oil painting is me. It is my baby that I'm constructing, and I'm putting my feelings on canvas."

"What would happen if Merrill suddenly went home to be with the Lord? Would you be able to cope with that situation?"

"I think so. I know I could. Not just with the loss but the thought of going through life alone. This wouldn't be easy. Maybe I'd stumble a bit along the way, but the Lord's with me. I must always remember that.

"We've discussed the future in this regard, you know. Merrill still flies a lot, whether in a private plane or commercially. At first, after he had recuperated well enough from the first accident, I asked him not to go back to a private plane. I didn't want to go through that nightmare again. He said, 'If it were a car accident, would you tell me not to ever get into a car again?' I said, 'No.' I knew I had lost the battle right there, so I didn't try to argue anymore. All I said was, 'When you do get another plane, then get it big enough, fast enough, powerful enough so that if you have another accident it'll make your own grave for you.' Before I didn't know what to expect from a burn victim. Now I do. I couldn't face a repeat. I think I'd start running and never stop.

Now, having said that, I know the Lord would help me adjust, but I do pray that it won't ever happen."

Criticism of Merrill hurts Virginia very much. After all, he is the man she loves. And when cynicism rears its ugly head in others, she becomes quite upset.

"I've heard that one criticism of Merrill's concerts is that he trades too much on his disability, as it were. Are you aware of this?"

"Yes, I've heard the same. I know some people feel this way. But I totally disregard them because the reason Merrill is out doing those concerts is that he's singing for the Lord. He's telling the story of why he has so much to praise God for. I feel sorry for people whose suspicions make them feel otherwise."

"But *why* do they do it? What compels them?" I asked.

"Because he has talent that they don't. He has ability they don't have. It's jealousy. They see him traveling—they think it's a glamourous life. But they don't realize that the glamour becomes tarnished after awhile. Merrill feels so very weary when he's traveling so much, but he continues to go on because his only purpose is to glorify the Lord. Merrill has been able to help hundreds and hundreds and hundreds, even thousands, through his testimony. We'll never know just how many until we get to Heaven."

"Does Merrill think often about death? It has been said that Billy Graham is doing so a lot lately. Ruth confirmed this during our interview. Does Merrill wonder how many years are left?"

"Yes. He's living on borrowed time, and he knows it. At the pace he's going, the way his body has been punished and tortured and abused so totally, he could go anytime. He doesn't feel that he's going to live to a ripe old age in any event, because none of the men in his family have done so. The oldest, I believe, is sixty-two years of age. So he feels that death may be just around the corner. And though it may come soon, he doesn't want to slow down, to rust out. He'll burn out, yes, but not rust. He'll drop in his tracks. This is what he wants to do. He doesn't want to sit back and waste time, but rather, redeem that time for Christ."

She looked at me intently as she said, "You know, Roger, I'm proud of my husband. I admire his talent, his growth as a Christian—the ministry he has, which is totally unique."

"Now, if you could just be proud of yourself, Virginia," I said softly, sincerely.

"I'm getting there," she replied, smiling. "I'm getting there."

She doesn't blame *anyone*; she holds no animosity toward *anyone*.

"It's just life," she said frankly. "It's how things turn out. So much of life seems geared toward making you feel inferior, subtly or otherwise. You let someone else go through a door first. It's always the other person first. In my case I always felt I was to be pushing others in front of me, and I was always to step behind them, stay in the background."

"What with the condo and the car and all the rest, isn't there a danger that you'll come to depend upon material things for your self-image, your self-respect? Are you concerned that coming here to Hawaii might be an escape instead of an attempt to find yourself?"

"No, really, there isn't that danger. I would gladly sell everything I've got and start again in a little tiny two-room house if that was what God wanted me to do."

Virginia is a woman of great strength as well as great weakness. When someone needs her, she is there, giving every second of time, every bit of effort required to help out. Ironically, the years following the crash might have crushed someone else. But, as she's said, because she was useful then, needed, an indispensable part of Merrill's survival and readjustment, the complex from which she suffers was glossed over or temporarily brushed aside.

Example: "Because of the fact that his face was deformed, I found it at first difficult to kiss him. But in time that came naturally to me. I learned to accept and to kiss his face. He was my husband, however he looked. The appearance he had was only on the surface. I knew what the man underneath was like."

Merrill himself felt, initially, perhaps as awkward as did Virginia.

"I remember one time he said to me, 'Virginia, how can you stay beside me when I look like this?' He must have been thinking that he was no longer attractive, *couldn't* be attractive due to the scars and such. And so I helped him through that inner crisis."

But when he was well, and then out on the road again, the waves of inferiority started to batter her once more.

. . . *so much of life is geared toward making you feel inferior.*

To a degree she is right. (Though someone with Virginia's complex will *look* for reasons that may be, in the final analysis, specious in her regard. There is a kind of comfort to be derived from sensing in life conditions that can affect not only her but others as well.)

Just watch TV during any prime time evening period. What do you see? Attractive people extolling the virtues of pain relievers, laxatives, toothpaste, automobiles, whatever. A false image is set up, piped into receivers that are capable of storing up these images for many, many years to come. Those "receivers" are you, me, Virginia, all of us who have a TV set in our homes and who watch it even infrequently.

It's the same in magazines: physically handsome people pushing cigarettes, cameras, liquor, and so on. Is your husband that hairy-chested, rugged-looking macho guy before whom all women are supposed to fall, panting?

Unlikely.

Your husband may even be bald. He may be overweight. There could be complexion problems inherited from his acne days as a teenager. He might wear glasses, be totally unathletic, and you might find him only so-so as a sex partner. (Perhaps he's even impotent.)

Sometimes that stain on that white dress shirt *won't* come out, despite how much "Name Brand" you use. Your dentures continue to be loose regardless of what substance is "guaranteed" on TV to relieve the problem. On and on. The reality of everyday existence clashing with the fabrications of behavior-inducing techniques via commercials on the air and in print.

Virginia will conquer this legacy of personal worthlessness. She is a Christian without compromise. She stands firm in all the essential doctrines. Christ has indeed been her Savior, her Redeemer for a long, long time. He will become, totally, her *Lord* when she emerges from the twisted, dented, battered cocoon in which she has been entrapped and which, for some, would be their coffin instead. The comparison is valid: A caterpillar can only crawl, and is susceptible to being stepped on by unknowing feet. But a butterfly is free; it can soar; it can reach up, one could fantasize, to the sky and beyond, to the gates of Heaven.

Marion Lindsell

Emotion tends to weaken ties with Scripture. Only the mind, the intellect, can grasp, in depth, much that God wants us to understand. How can we understand eschatology only on an emotional level? How can we grasp the concepts of the virgin birth and such a great deal else strictly through the "eyes" of our emotions.

The foregoing is why I was eager to meet Dr. Harold Lindsell, the man who defended inerrancy in his classic book, *Battle for the Bible*. (Inerrancy is yet another example of a doctrine, a concept, that cannot be defended on the basis of emotional ecstasy, but which requires the intellectual capacity that is as much a "gift" from God as any other.)

I was delighted with the prospect of meeting his wife, Marion. A number of people had recommended her very highly. Harold was kind enough to mention this book to her, and she consented to an interview.

Following is the text of that interview . . .

How many children do you have?

Four. I had the total responsibility for them because of a very busy husband who was gone a great deal. The struggle of raising the children was the hardest part, trying to be wise and kind when sometimes you are very low physically.

What made it all worse for me was that, during a period of fifteen years, I had had four surgeries. While all this was going on, I had the children at home. None of them had moved away as yet.

Coincident with my gall bladder surgery, for instance, two of them came down with chicken pox. But you learn to cope with such events day by day. The Lord somehow gives you strength.

Your health has never been what you would call robust?

That's right. I have had a lot of problems over the years. I have felt, at times, that my body was always recuperating, always catching up, that I have never really gotten quite on top of things physically.

There was so much that didn't *have* to happen. I had surgery the year after John was born, and they left a stone in the common duct. After awhile I began having those pains all over again. It was an accident, sloppy surgery. So I had to have another operation five years later. I was so sick. And then there was the cancer surgery. And then a hysterectomy in 1970.

What would you say is alarming in society as concerns children?

I think our second daughter Joanne put her finger on it pretty accurately. She said she went through her college days before the drug problem became real pronounced, and that the same was true of the permissiveness in sexual life. But nowadays these are so prominent. I'd have to say that both are alarming trends.

I think the hardest thing to face today in bringing up children is the constant, constant watch care over their honesty, even the little things that day by day you can't let pass by. You can't allow them to get away with *any* dishonesty.

We have always been very open with our children. I'm sure some people would be shocked to sit at our table and listen to some of the dinner conversations. Our youngsters have a very outspoken way; they're all very vocal. While we have never allowed them to be disrespectful, at the same time we have certainly encouraged them to express their opinions and sometimes these are very wild.

But this means that we have always talked everything out. We have never harbored anything inside. Dishonesty is what turns youngsters off more quickly than anything. Hypocrisy. So many Christians are one type of person outside the home, and entirely different inside the home.

Consistency is so important. I remember one time when Harold was bringing the children home and stopped to get a loaf of bread. Partway home he discovered that the clerk had given him three cents too much change back. So he stopped the car, turned around, went back, and gave the man the three cents. The children have never fogotten that. It's a tiny incident and yet it was something that showed them how honest their father was.

Such incidents affect what will happen when they leave home to go out on their own. Will they be effective soul winners? After all, God has no grandchildren, you know.

But even at our best we find that our children want to change a bit from the way their parents are. I mean, John and his wife are so much more into the simple life-style than Harold and I are.

What do they find wrong with your life-style?

They think perhaps we're too materialistic. We get a new car when the old one is not quite up to snuff, rather than making it last until its last gasp. We get new furniture when the old becomes fairly worn, rather than keeping it until it falls apart. Their idea is that the money spent could be given to World Vision, for example, to help the hungry people of the world.

If you discovered that you had only a short time left to live, what difference would this make in your life? How do you think your children would treat you?

Anyone who has had cancer faces such thoughts. My mother had both breasts removed. My cousin in Florida had one removed. My two aunts died of breast cancer, and my mother died of a related disease which they think she got from all the radiation she had. I used to pray, "Dear Lord, let me see my children married to Christians, and let me see my grandchildren." Well, all that has happened and so I don't know how much more I can ask for.

As for how the children would treat me, I think they would come to see us more often. But if we conduct our lives differently after finding out about something along these lines, aren't we being a bit hypocritical?

Would Harold be able to function if you went first?

I think so, yes. We're very pragmatic about the possibility. We talk about it. I'll say, 'Honey, if something were to happen to me right now, what would you do?' (When he had his lung collapse years ago, I thought I'd be the one left.) Then there have been my operations. Just recently, in fact, we thought I had bone cancer. It turned out to be arthritis. I had a bone scan which confirmed this, but the pains didn't seem like those that would come from arthritis. So we've had to confront the possibility of death a number of times. We never run from it in denial. Those who do are guaranteeing a confused and draining period of unnecessary anxiety for the loved one who survives. Harold and I love each other so much that we want the aftereffects of death to be minimized.

Beverly LaHaye

Nightmares come without warning. They may be based upon nothing more than seeing a horrible picture in a newspaper, perhaps of a tragic plane crash. It upsets us. We are sorrowful over the dead, concerned over the injured. We go to sleep with certain images that have gradually slipped down just below the top "layer" of our subconscious.

A nightmare ensues. Usually it is not repeated. Usually it literally comes and goes—and our lives do not know its imprint for longer than a very brief, transitory period.

But nightmares, for millions of Americans—Christian or otherwise—can be indicative of deep-seated problems in their lives. Their worst fears, too ugly and frightening for conscious and open discussion, come to a head at night, screeching through the still air with the cries of our anguish as we awaken from them, our bodies shuddering.

Take this nightmare, for example:

"I am very old, very ill. My body is a swelling mass of pain. I

157

have very little money. I climb the stairs to a seedy little apartment on the second floor of a decaying building. The carpet runner is little more than ragged bunches of long-ago useless material. There is dust everywhere. I cough a little, pain ricocheting through me.

"I reach my apartment door, fumble for the key, unlock the door, open it, go inside, shut the door, and lock it again. I have been to the corner pharmacy to get some more medicine.

"I go to the single window in this living room/dining room area of the apartment, and look out. So little to see. People going by don't know I exist. Nobody does.

"I sit down on a chair which is next to a round table. On top of the table is a phone. I fall back, so tired—tired of life, tired of loneliness, tired of sitting there and waiting for the call that will never come. It will never come because no one cares whether I live or die."

This nightmare is the sort that might well come to an overly protected child, an only child who has been cushioned from the outside world by his well-meaning but possessive parents. When they die, he is left without a lifelong anchor.

Being an only child was discussed candidly with Beverly LaHaye. She has counseled with the former type of young person and/or his parents. She has become increasingly concerned over trends in the latter.

"Do you think being an only child is really such a handicap, Beverly?" I asked. "Or has it been blown out of all proportion to reality over the years?"

"It depends upon the parents," she replied. "My daughter married an only child and he is a very well-adjusted adult. His parents, real wisely, treated him in the right way, without giving him all the things in the world that he wanted. They disciplined him and loved him and yet they kept him in touch with other young people. He grew up in a church with plenty of youth activities. You'd really never *know* he was an only kid."

"If you were fellowshipping with somebody for a couple of hours or so, and you didn't know anything about this person's background, could you tell whether he was an only child or not?"

"I've done that, yes. It shows in whether they seem to be demanding or not, whether they have a bent toward always having their own way. When you get an extreme like that, I think you can spot him pretty easily."

"Do only children, generally, have more emotional problems, whether or not these are conquered not being the issue here?"

"I have to ask myself the question, 'Would that same child have the problems he has if there had been three other kids in the same family? Is it the parents, the child himself, the environment?' And there are so many variables. But it does require an extra effort on the parents' part. It takes wise parents to bring up a single child."

"Now, Beverly, you counsel a great many mothers as a result of your involvement with Family Life Seminars. Are there two or three problems in their relationships with their offspring that seem to be the most prevalent?"

"One that stands out in my mind is the question of whether or not a mother should expect her children to follow her rules and regulations to the final comma and period. Or should she give them gradually increasing liberty and freedom?"

"Restrictive as opposed to permissive."

"Yes, right. That seems to be a problem encountered often when we've met with mothers—and fathers, too. I get a lot of mail about the intricacies of raising children. A lot of it.

" 'How much must a parent insist upon children doing what the parents wish? Where's the line, the break off point?' What I advocate is threefold: You need love; you need instruction; and you need the determination to insist upon rules/instructions being followed until you, the parent, decide when to loosen up things a bit."

"What about discipline as an issue?" I asked at this point. "Do you feel that physical punishment is okay?"

"Yes, if it's applied with love. I think Proverbs makes that quite clear. Yet, whenever you talk about punishment, people today immediately think, 'Oh, child abuse. It's a borderline child abuse. We parents shouldn't be striking our children.' But Proverbs talks about the use of the rod in correction. I think it's all tied in with love, motive. Hebrews 12 gives the example of the heavenly Father disciplining those whom He loves."

"But punishment may be the wrong word here, don't you think? Aren't we really talking about chastisement? Punishment is pretty much a dead-end kind of thing. But chastisement is with the purpose of correction, and instruction."

"That's right—the intention is to change the behavior to a more acceptable pattern."

"Do you have many parents coming to you with their children trapped in homosexual behavior?"

"We have some, yes. Most of the letters we get are from homosexuals themselves—kids who read Tim's book on the subject who were so relieved and who had a fresh, hopeful outlook that they could change their way of life. Before they had been brainwashed into thinking that, once gay, always gay.

"The parents of kids who are homosexual write to us, asking, 'What can we do? What shall we do?' We have several clinics across the country which we recommend for them to visit and obtain counseling. It is counseling for the parents, because they, too, have to learn how to cope with the situation, and what to do to help their youngster."

Just as this chapter was being written, I happened to take a break for a moment and turned on the television. One of the current crop of rock singers was on. Since I abhor the stuff, Christianized or not, I was reaching to flick to another channel when I hesitated for a moment. Male or female? I looked, thought, couldn't decide. I did not know which sex the singer was!

That is just the example being force-fed into the minds of young people today. The record industry is booming—$40,000,000,000 annually at present. Ninety percent or more of the songs are garbage musically or morally or both. One recent report said that young people often give up food to buy a current single or long-playing album. They rush home, or to their college apartments, plug in the earphones, turn on the psychedelic lighting, and enter another world, a world of suggestive sexual and drug lyrics.

Want a prediction? Within three years after you have finished reading this book, you will have heard much indeed about the first hard-rock gay album. It will be accepted with hardly a ripple in the secular community. What Christians will do remains to be seen.

The Year of the Child.

Beverly LaHaye is one of a growing list of Christian mothers who have been/are being alerted to the Frankensteinian monster that could be embodied by this term.

The Year of the Child.

It sounds awfully good, noble, a much-needed development to overcome the damage done to young minds in this decade.

It . . . *isn't any of those things.*

"In the matter of child abuse, Beverly," I asked, "is it really as much of a problem as the media seem to be indicating?"

"Well, you've touched a sore spot, Roger. I know it *is* a problem. I know there are thousands of kids who *are* mistreated—but I think the media has blown it all *way* out of perspective."

"They grab ahold of something and milk it for all it's worth."

"Exactly. I suspect they're preparing us for the Year of the Child commencement, and brainwashing us for the aftermath that will follow for a long time to come. President Carter appointed a commission of more than twenty individuals to direct its activities. You'd be appalled to know who some of the appointees are."

"Timothy O'Leary perhaps," I laughed sardonically, thinking of the leader of the drug culture years ago. He has in recent years allegedly gone respectable, but he still advocates turning on to the pleasures of the various drugs.

"Almost as bad. They're gearing up toward control of the family. Through ERA they're chipping away at the foundation of the home. I predict that when everything is clear we will see the precedent being set for taking away and controlling our children. The parents will no longer have any say, at least the natural parents.

"Tim and I traveled in Sweden two years ago and saw what has happened there. A child, when the parents spank him, can go to the authorities and say, 'My parents are abusing me. I want to be removed from their home.' The government will pull that child out of the home and take care of him until he gets to the age when he can be self-supporting.

"We talked to one beautiful nineteen-year-old girl who was spanked when she was thirteen because she had done something very wrong. She was so hostile toward her father, who had done the spanking, she went to the authorities and complained. So the government took her out of the home, put her in a child-care center where the government controlled everything she did, and gave her an allowance. She ultimately tried every sin known in the book. By the time she was eighteen, she had almost destroyed her life. But she was met by a Campus Crusade worker who led her to Jesus Christ. When we spoke to her, she was happy but concerned about the future. She had one very poignant question that Tim and I shall never forget: 'With the past life that I've lived, is there any hope for me ever to have a happy marriage?' Well, that is what control by government does; that is what happens when control is taken out of the parents' hands."

"Sounds Russian," I observed.

And it surely did. I was reminded of that verse in Romans 1 which tells of God giving them over to a reprobate mind. That's what happens when Christian parents are no longer able to have any say in the rearing-up-a-child-in-the-way-he-should-go process. When institutions take over, Hell almost literally breaks loose. Even Ruth Graham had her faith weakened by a young man who'd had *his* faith *destroyed* while attending a secular university.

Furthermore, what kind of world does government send these kids out into after removing the anchor of Christ from their lives or blocking that anchor from ever entering in the first place?

God's Word tells me that the wisdom of God is as foolishness to men. Divine truths are ridiculed, then cast aside. Born-again Christianity is often grist for the situation comedy mill on television.

Other "values" promulgated on television seem more suited for the locker room than the living room. The daughter of a prominent born-again celebrity of long-standing rationalizes herself into appearing on a disco dance series—presenting this as an example to other young people.

Beverly said: "I think we're in the latter days, Roger. We're very near the return of our beloved Lord."

The sensual atmosphere of the disco. Oh, don't be so hard on young people, we're told. They're just having a good time. But disco dancing is show-off dancing, blatantly erotic at times. Disco dancing comes alive in a swirling place of clashing colored lights and ear-bursting music and—

She continued: "It's all so satanic. Tim and I believe that fully. An atmosphere of hate and fear and mistrust in and of children/young people is being created, so that it's going to be easier to come in and take them away 'for their own good.' "

So many *products* now have the capability of bringing into being veritable armies of disturbed, distorted, grotesque minds and bodies. Birth control pills can cause mongoloidism. Cigarette smoking can foster weak hearts and lungs in the unborn. Upper and downer pills. Foods with preservatives. On and on the list extends. Is it all based upon the greed of the manufacturers? Their stupidity?

162

"Think of our world right now, Roger, and then try to imagine how different conditions were fifty years ago. Think about what we tolerate today, and then realize what would have been outlawed half a century ago. How devious most of it is. Under the guise of ERA lesbians are going to gain such a great deal. Under the guise of protecting children, those very children are going to be destroyed in the long run."

Teenagers jumping off bridges, strung out on drugs. Mongoloids in institutions, gazing out at a bewildering environment, wanting to express so much but unable to do so. Their pathetic minds made that way by smoking or drinking or pills or foods with preservatives or all of these together, the diet of their mothers.

You get a chill when you think of these things. But what you feel as a convicted born-again Christian mother is nothing, as it were, to what lies in store for those responsible.

The words were spoken softly but contained a hard lesson. God Incarnate, a child on His lap, His hand running gently through that child's soft, soft hair. What He said was directed at all of mankind for all the centuries of time to follow: "Woe unto him who causes these little ones to stumble. It would be better for him that he never have been born, or that a millstone be hanged about his neck and that he be cast into the deepest sea."

Betty Robison

James Robison is one of the most profoundly dynamic preachers I have ever met. Some evangelical insiders say that he may well become the next Billy Graham. Others will insist that he is *too* conservative. Certainly his fundamental approach to Scripture was evidenced some time ago when one Texas television station dropped his program because he attacked a minority. That minority happened to be homosexuals, and James told what was an inescapable Biblical truth about them.

His wife Betty is no exception. Her stance on life's issues is conservative as well. She seems to be the perfect helpmate for this talented and energetic evangelist from Fort Worth-Dallas.

With James away so much, on crusades and other meetings, how do you cope with being both mother and father to your youngsters?

It's a great responsibility, it really is. But I feel that the Lord called me to render a special service, that is, to be an evangelist's wife. It's just a matter of daily yielding yourself to Him, for His total guidance. Physically, psychologically I am not in myself capable. It is only in and through Him that I am able to get along.

Teenage girls today seem predisposed toward immodesty, especially in their attire. Are you concerned about this in your own home?

Yes, we are. We've tried to teach modesty and such in our family, instilling in Teresa the need to respect her body, that—as a Christian—she has a responsibility to magnify the Lord. The way she dresses is one aspect of this. If she is immodest, un-Christlike, that hurts her testimony, makes her witness ineffectual. She sets an example even in front of those watching her who are not Christians.

What concerns you most as a wife and mother?

I want to be the right kind of wife and mother. I want to please my husband and do my best to raise the children as God wants them raised. But I don't sit and fret about any of this.

Early on, during the beginning years, I tended to be a very domineering person. But I've been changing since then. The Lord has done some great things in my life. If He had not given me the strong husband that James is, well, I might have had a harder time changing.

If you need something, material or otherwise, how do you approach James? Do you ever have to play tricks on him, manipulate him, as it were?

I'm completely honest with him, and he's very fair to me. I don't like the "getting what you want" syndrome of manipulating him or anyone else for that matter. I just tell James my needs and we pray about it all. If that's what we feel God wants me to have, we get it. If he says, after prayer and discussion. "No, I don't think you need that," I don't go out and pout and fret about it. He's the head of the home, the leader. I trust my husband completely. I trust him because I believe his relationship with the Lord is pure and right.

If I were a child in your family, would I be looking at you as pretty tough parents?

I don't think so. I hope that my children see me just as a

concerned mother who loves them very deeply. Nor is James, as you say, a tough father. They rightly love and respect their daddy. He's firm but he is loving. Children love discipline. Now, I know that seems hard to swallow, but it's true in the long run. Children who have known the right measure of discipline grow up to be adults who look back on their childhood with honest appreciation.

It's the attention that's important. If you're angry, you're wrong; that's a sin. But if you discipline them out of a broken heart, and out of love, they can tell the difference. I let them know *why* I am doing so. I actually say, "I don't want to do this. It doesn't make me happy. In fact, it breaks my heart, and I do love you very much." Normally, they will come back to me afterwards and hug me, and kiss me, and say, "I love you, Mother." Because they know I had no other choice in view of their actions.

Has becoming a mother been easy for you? Was giving birth a breeze, as the expression goes?

Not at all. After Rhonda's difficult delivery, the doctors told me that I could not have any more children. We were informed that my condition was such that the birth of Rhonda was a real miracle. So we decided to adopt since we did want a larger family. Randy then entered our life. He has been such a joy to us. He just fulfilled every dream I ever had of having another child. I couldn't love him any more if I had given birth to him. After we adopted Randy, I forgot about asking the Lord to let me have another child of my own.

Then I did become pregnant again, and Robin was born. This happened three years after Randy was brought home. But it was another difficult delivery. I almost had a miscarriage. After Robin was born she was just barely breathing. The doctors expected her to be retarded, or something else severely wrong with her. She is really a walking miracle because she is very normal, very bright.

Have you ever looked at other people and wished you could be like them?

I think it's natural for a person to see different qualities in others, and think, "I wished I could be like that, or do that." For example: I'm basically very quiet, not a great conversationalist, even a little timid. I meet people who are the opposite, and wish I could change and adopt a bit of their personality.

You and James believe very much in living separated lives. Isn't this more difficult now than it's ever been? Especially for your children?

Yes, it is tough. But our children are very stable, very grounded in the Bible. They're aware that they're Christians, and they have an obligation to honor their Lord. We're teaching them Christ-centered values, not worldly ones. Having things isn't going to make them happy, at least on a long-term basis. Living for Him is the answer, the important aspect of life. The Lord has given our oldest daughter a real burden for other kids at school. Nobody but Christ could have worked in her life at such an early stage, to make her look at her peers and want to give to them what she enjoys in Him.

Oh, my children do like some material things, of course; God gives us much that we can richly use and enjoy. But they don't look to the material for satisfaction

We do pray about even little matters. Should we buy that car? That refrigerator? Should I have that dress, that watch, whatever? We are totally the Lord's, and He is interested in every facet of our lives. Whether it's buying groceries or how much we should spend in other areas, God wants us to make the right decision, to include Him in everything. After all, the money we earn is His money, and we should use it wisely. In myself I'm not able to decide it all, so I go to Him and ask Him, because our wisdom is, in His eyes, mere foolishness.

Julia Staton

What mistakes that, in your opinion, seem common to most Christian mothers have you, yourself, fallen into?

I honestly think that I was warned in advance of having children. Before they came I had gotten real busy in the church. I learned, before it was too late, that I had to say no from time to time. As a minister's wife I guess I was trying to fulfill everybody else's expectation of what a minister's wife should be doing. I learned to place myself at the Lord's disposal, to be what *He* wanted, and not what others had preconceived in their minds.

How did you go about approaching your youngsters with the facts of life?

Randy was quite young when Rena was born, but he was a very alert, inquisitive child. He asked what was going on in my tummy. Even then he wanted to know whatever I was prepared, or Knofel was prepared, to tell him.

It was difficult for me, though. Probably because my parents didn't really explain anything to me. Until I was a teenager I never asked any questions at all. When I did my mother seemed reluctant to answer and I had to do the approaching.

As a result of not having had my parents candid about sex, I determined to avoid this same trap with my own children. I found it difficult, at first, to express the candor I felt was necessary. But I did become blunt with them. Whenever they hear anything on TV, or at school, they come to me, and I explain the situation as well as I can.

Some people would not agree with the way we conduct family life. For example, when Randy asked about why he had a penis, we did call that and other parts of the body by what they *are* called. It's not dirty or profane to use the medical terms. A breast *is* a breast. Your ears *are* your ears. There are really only certain *correct* words to use. So we've always used vagina, etc. in response to the children's questions.

I remember one time that Randy walked in on Knofel and myself in the bedroom when we were making love. This did, of course, lead to questions in his mind. Later, we simply told him we were making love. We explained that when two persons are in love, they have sex. This relationship is to occur for them only within marriage, and it often leads to babies. It was how Randy and his sister came into being.

Have you ever discussed such areas as masturbation? How would you have done so?

I've not talked about this with them. But Knofel has mentioned it to Randy. Our son has never shown any interest, and so the subject isn't a prominent one by any means.

We have talked about homosexuality, though. Randy's heard the word a lot, and he wanted to know what it was all about. We have explained to him that he must be very careful with men, especially strangers who may get too chummy. We have explained that his body is very precious, is to be kept solely for him and his wife, and no one else is to bother him in that way.

I think the aversion of some parents to honesty about sex, that it is a hush-hush situation, makes it shady to youngsters. This can contribute to perversion later on, in my opinion.

We have a sick world, Julia. We hear daily of homosexuality, abortion, sex change operations, pornography, and so much else.

It's becoming a torrent. Have you ever thought that it's better not to bring up children because of the moral and spiritual cesspool which they must enter eventually?

No. My children are going to be influences against those conditions. I think that Christians are *compelled* to people the world, to try and counteract the immorality, the decay. If we are going to say, 'I don't want my children living in that kind of world,' then we are detracting from the influence that Christ can have. I can't go to the mission field and preach to the natives or go into the slums or wherever, but I have four children in my home. Maybe one of them can go, or they all can be an influence in the school and, sooner or later, whatever work they choose to do.

You sound very much together, Julia, as the modern expression says. But, frankly, where are you a bad example? Where do you fall short as a mother?

I yell a lot. Instead of going into the room where the children are, I yell from another room, maybe the kitchen into the living room. That is very annoying to them, to anyone.

Do they yell back?

Yes, unfortunately. They learned it from me. Sometimes we all fall into the quicksand of inconsistency, and children are quick to pick this up.

Occasionally I feel very tired and have a headache and am a little touchy as a result. My children understand this, because they have such moments, too. And I am trying, hard, to overcome my bad habits, to handle myself better.

There are times when I feel pressure to get to some place exactly on time or get some particular task done quickly. If the children are involved, I say, 'Hurry up! Get that dress on! Get that hair combed! What are you doing just standing around? Don't you know we're going to be late if we don't step on it? Hurry! Hurry!' This is wrong. It imparts anxiety. It leads to irritation. It builds frustration.

But I recognize where I am weak, where I need to change. And we are very supportive of one another in this family. We help one another. We strengthen one another.

What are some of the special joys of motherhood, Julia?

Watching my children grow, and develop, and become their

own distinct individuals. I feel great closeness, affection between us. There is real confidence within me that the children are going to be good additions to the world, that they are going to help the cause of Christ.

These are the basics as far as I am concerned. Family ties, the security of the family, the lifelong love and devotion—these are very real, very important to me.

Marabel Morgan

Have you ever noticed how happy some people seemingly feel all the time? No matter what time of day, they've got a sunny smile on their face, and their manner is "up."

But there's no guarantee that the smile on the outside doesn't mask anguish on the inside. The old line, "Nobody knows the trouble I see," can be a bulls-eye arrow in terms of hitting the truth.

Nobody knows. . . .

Except the ones who are suffering. Can you imagine what it's like to have to smile, with apparent Christian joy, when your heart is breaking? To smile when you have just lost a child soon after its birth, a child for which you prayed and which has now been taken from you?

Marabel Morgan knows, all too well.

How did she die, Marabel?

"Her little lungs just collapsed," Marabel says, her voice breaking a little.

What did you name one who lived for so short a time?

"We never did name her."

So brief a life. Not yet a personality—not in fact, never in recollection. The child was tiny, the fingers hardly formed. In Marabel's womb, this child seemed safe, warm, unconcerned about entrance into the outer world, unaware of anything but its cozy environment, and only vaguely so of that.

And then the child was born. And then the child died.

Only three days of life for that fragile little baby, totally helpless, weren't materially different from the months inside Marabel's body. At least it can be hoped that this was the case. Perhaps a fleeting perception, a brief intrusion inside the infant consciousness, but that was the extent.

Months of recuperation for Marabel and Charlie; groping to accept the justice of what had happened; trying hard not to have their faith denied; opening themselves before the God of the universe and honestly, honestly asking, "Help us, O Lord. Please help us."

And He did.

They survived and emerged from the mourning that followed the death of their three-day-old, unnamed but loved, little one. After facing the inevitable questions of why, they secured answers in prayer and trust.

And then it all appeared to be happening over again.

"Michelle was born prematurely, too," Marabel recalls. "Her lungs collapsed. She didn't even weigh six pounds. The doctors went in this time and operated on her. They had never before operated on a day-old baby, but not to have done so would have guaranteed the death of Michelle.

"They blew up her lungs and, a day or so later, the lungs collapsed again. We thought surely that we were going to lose Michelle. But after another major operation, and weeks of waiting, her condition stabilized."

And, today, the Morgans have another daughter, Laura, in addition to Michelle.

Do you ever think about your first child? Do you feel as deeply about her as one that has lived a number of years?

"I think about that child every so often," Marabel replies. "Having had that experience has made me approach with much more insight and sympathy women who have undergone something similar. I used to think, 'Oh, my word, those women . . . why do they act like that? They didn't get to know the child.' "

Have you ever seen Marabel in person? Have you ever walked up to her and introduced yourself and seen that smile of hers? Have you ever realized the triumph behind it?

"Problems don't go away," she continued. "I have many cares even now. If I didn't, I'd be six feet under. Everybody has cares, heartaches. But the Lord takes charge of things for us. If we surrender to Him, He helps us, gives the courage to meet tomorrow."

To interview Marabel Morgan is inevitably to face the question of her *Total Woman* ministry. Critics will say that she puts sex ahead of virtually all other marital considerations. A flip reply by Marabel would be: "Oh, have you not read The Song of Solomon?"

But Marabel is not flippant. She is a deeply caring, sensitive woman.

"The Lord talks about His church and himself, comparing this relationship to that of marriage. What sets the marriage relationship apart from, say, a partnership in business? It's the sexual act. So I think the Lord is talking about the closeness, the intimacy of marriage—a physical portrayal on earth of what life is like in Heaven."

How are you going about the task of opening the eyes of your daughters to the sexual part of life?

"My daughters know that I try to be really jazzy in my own bedroom with my own husband. I wouldn't meet Charlie at the door in see-through Saran Wrap if my daughters were looking on, but I try to tell them, as best I can, what marriage from the sexual perspective should be with a husband.

"So many TV programs have something questionable/immoral these days. I try to explain what is right to them. I say, 'This is the world's style. They act this way to entice one another, to seduce and tarnish what God intended only for husband and wife. As a result they'll never have the peace and security of knowing what God can bring to a man and a woman in marriage. Isn't it interesting that what the world does, sexually, outside of marriage is what the Lord can transform within marriage and bring such joy and fun as a result.'

"Now I don't know if I'm doing this right or not, but I'm trying the best way I can. I'm doing a lot of talking and they're listening.

174

They see that Charlie and I are so excited about each other, not just sexually, but on an overall basis—just so content and happy when we're together.

"When we celebrated our fifteenth anniversary, and were sitting at the table laughing and talking, I reached over and said to Charlie that I loved him and ruffled his hair and hugged him a little bit. The girls grinned and went right on eating. It's natural for all of us. But I've talked with many, many women who say they can never remember their mother and father even once touching or kissing each other."

Even in view of the foregoing, there are those who criticize Marabel. They try to point out how wrong the direction of her ministry is.

But for Marabel only one answer is possible.

"What choice do I have? Christ is my Master, and if He says to do it, as I believe He has, I've got to do it. He led me to write *Total Woman*. I did expect a lot of guff. In fact, I'm going to tell you very honestly how I felt. When I was writing down some of those things in my bedroom, I thought to myself, 'Lord, if I write what I feel You want me to write, I won't be able to go to the grocery store again. I'll never be able to show my face in public. The Christian community may write me off.' And it seemed to me, as I read His Word, and prayed, that He was saying, 'Write it, write it.'

"So I did. I'm not ashamed of anything I wrote. As I said to one person, 'Why should we be ashamed to talk about what God wasn't ashamed to create?' "

Would you give up this ministry, however, if you felt God wanted you to do something else?

"Without hesitation. I think that God just loves to intervene in people's lives when they think they've got it all put together. He just loves to turn things around and send them out on a different path.

"I've seen it happen. So I don't think there is anything sacred about a specific type of ministry or a ministry under a certain name. If the Lord were to say, 'Now, Marabel, we're going to be doing something different,' I would follow Him. I just want to get the gospel out however I am able to do so."

Jeanette Myra

Jeanette Myra, mother of a nine-year-old girl and six- and three-year-old boys, loves her role. Her husband Harold, president of Christianity Today, an influential Christian magazine publisher, appreciates the blessings of being married.

"We constantly communicate to one another," she told me in the living room of their Wheaton, Illinois, home, Harold sitting nearby. "We share. Communication is essential to a happy marriage."

Oh, yes! But these days there isn't enough of it, so to speak. Lives are compartmentalized, rather like two suites in a hotel or motel with no connecting door between them.

"Harold asks my advice often," Jeanette remarked. "I have strong opinions. So does he. We express these to one another."

"Where do you feel the most qualified to help him?" I asked.

"Let's say the relationships between members of the staff, human relationships. Are people happy working there? Were they upset by one person leaving? How do they relate to the new one?

Gloria Gaither

Patricia MacArthur

Betty Robison

Margaret Taylor

Dorothy Engstrom

Vonette Bright

Shirley Dobson

Doris Moody

Joan Winmill Brown

Nellie Connally

Marabel Morgan

"Harold brings a degree of the office home with him. I want it that way. Anything else wouldn't work in this family. Even though this is against the classic formulas about peace in the family, in our case I think we have a lot more peace because of it."

"Now, we've established that he asks you for advice. What about the other way around?"

"Oh, yes! All the time. We discuss matters dealing with raising the kids, including school. Should I talk to the principal about this problem or shouldn't I? Nitty-gritty stuff like, should I sign Michelle up for lessons at the Y or is it too much of a pain to drive her over there? I mean we really do spend hours this way."

Harold interpolated at this point that "Constant talking is required for a good marital relationship. It's as if someone tried to run a business without a lot of talking between the managers of the business. To run a marriage without an awful lot of discussion, well, we don't feel it can be done successfully."

Jeanette added, candidly, "Some men are very bored by matters that have to do with the household. Sometimes I think Harold isn't really interested in whether Michelle or Todd takes lessons at the Y. But they're half his children and it's our responsibility to discuss these matters. For one thing, they might cost money and he's making the money in this house. I'd better be sure he approves what I'm doing with it."

Earlier Harold and I had been talking, at lunch actually, and he mentioned that walking across the street to shake hands with the President of the United States or going overseas to visit the Eiffel Tower or whatever wouldn't particularly thrill him. He preferred reading or working with people.

Knowing this I asked him, "Do you then find that you have to force yourself to be interested in more mundane matters of family life?"

"Sometimes," he acknowledged. "But I think that it's more important for me to talk to my son than it is to talk to the President. I mean, I would be a blip on President Carter's day if I happened to be walking through a receiving line. But as far as my son is concerned, it is extremely important to him what kind of father image I provide for him. Running off overseas is very insignificant alongside of sitting and playing with a grasshopper in the presence of my son."

"What about when your son or your daughter brings you a tattered sheet of paper with some scrawl. It is presented as their conception of a bird or a dog or a horse. You have to somehow praise a work that is, by the lowest professional standards, atrocious. How do you respond honestly?"

"A parent sees it through his own parental, loving eyes," Harold replied. "To that parent it's good when taken at the level of the child's ability and creativity.

"If you're looking at that painting on the wall, there is no comparison. But this is your own flesh and blood. I personally couldn't care less about the crazy little scrawls done by someone else's child. But there is some kind of fantastic emotion between a parent and his child. You care so much about that child's feelings. You love that child so much and you're watching that child develop day by day. First you see that the child is able to hang onto a crayon, which is an exciting thing for a youngster, let alone do *anything* with it. Look, my son, my daughter, they can hang onto that crayon. You think it's cute. You think it's really special. Because it's *your* little person.

"And then they learn to make a mark. They're so excited that they can make a mark on paper. You are excited with them. Then it's the feeling of you wanting them to feel good about what they're doing. So you say something like, 'Oh, you chose beautiful colors. Oh, I love this purple.' All of that *is* true. There is no lie involved. Or you might say, 'Oh, you had a great time drawing that, didn't you? Or: 'That's very interesting, tell me about it.' It's very natural, because you love the child.

"I recall an experience I had when Michelle was about four." Jeanette said. "I took her to the beauty shop to have her hair cut in a different style and a little bit shorter. I sat and watched her get her hair cut. It happened to be a style that I had had when I was her age. All of a sudden, I looked at her and she seemed to be just like I was, a duplicate of me. A wave of empathy and love came over me, and it still does when I look at her and relate to her. It's like relating to me when I was a child.

"I think I'm very strict with the children, by the way. I think I exercise pretty tight control over them. If there isn't this control, and punishment when necessary, you suffer the natural consequences later on. That's the way life is. That's the way it is."

"Do you ever worry about the future, Jeanette?" I asked. "Do you ever wonder if you'll be wise enough to do the right job, so that, at the point your children enter the world, you won't have to worry so much about *their* future?"

"Everyday," she said. "I hope I won't be so cocky as to think I am doing everything precisely right. Sure, I worry about what's going to happen. I worry when they go to kindergarten because of the influences there. We try to set an example within the home, but on the outside, it's entirely another matter."

Harold added, "We need to leave our children to God, in a sense. While still doing our best. Because if we worry unduly, we're going to drive ourselves into an unnecessary frazzle. We have to realize that our children have their own problems. Parents often take these as their own. But the problems of our children, especially when they are close to growing up, are theirs. Now, I'm not saying that parents shouldn't love their children, be a counselor to them, give leadership to them. But not so much as they approach adulthood, because then they must learn to solve their own problems."

Jeanette went on with perhaps the single most crucial factor of all: "I really do completely believe that God is in control of every thing. So, if something traumatic happens to my child, at school, for instance, I absolutely, firmly believe that God knows all about it—that it is going to work out to His glory, whatever the outcome."

We switched to some reflection about marriage itself. Jeanette and Harold seemed exceptionally happy "together." I wanted to find out more of what was in the success formula which they apparently were embracing.

"Let's say," I began, "that this is actually ten or twelve years from now and Michelle is about to get married. Would you give her, as a book to help her, Marabel Morgan's *Total Woman?*"

"I appreciate a lot of her ideas. Her critics say that she advocates manipulating her husband. Aren't we all guilty of that, to a degree? It happens in every marriage, consciously or otherwise."

She pointed to the rather beautiful coffee table in front of us.

"See that?" she said. "He didn't think I should have it, and I really wanted it. I thought it was the perfect thing for this room, and this went on for some time. Finally, one day, I told him, 'Look, Harold, I'll give you an hour and a half of back rubs if you let me get that table.' I can get my husband to do just about anything if I promise him those back rubs. He's crazy about them!"

We both were laughing at this point. (I can't remember if Harold was.)

"Really," she said after a bit, "I want our relationship to be a very long and satisfying one for both of us. I want him to be a happily married man. And there are some things that just really please him. You know, people emphasize the sexual part of married life, but there is ever so much more. Every person is unique. Every person is made content by a variety of different influences, factors.

"Harold has helped me so much as a person. When we were dating, he used to say, 'Come on, assert yourself.' I was very quiet, mousy, and he would say, 'Where would you like to go?' It ended up with him always making the decision. But he soon got my self-confidence up. I guess he wishes he never had, because I've not shut up since then!"

"We respect each other's intelligence," Harold said. "She will have many insights, intuitive or otherwise, that I won't have. So it's a very complementary relationship. She'll see things that I don't see. And hopefully I'll see things that she doesn't. We work *together*, and that's what the partnership is all about."

They have a great deal going for them, these two.

"It scares me sometimes," Jeanette said frankly. "Because I am very contented, satisfied. Everything is perfect. I have three children, healthy and hopefully happy. And a very kind husband.

"But what if my child, any of them, had been born retarded? What if I had to live in a little shack and had no friends? What if any of these or more were part and parcel of my life? I have every *reason*, now, to be happy. But what about in other circumstances?"

"Are you concerned that your contentment may be disproportionately from material, physical things, circumstances?"

"I've never been tested. It's scary sometimes."

"We've been so blessed," Harold interjected. "A couple of nights ago we were upstairs and Greg was sound asleep. It was the middle of the night and we were just staring down at him, seeing his little body. Well, there is such great joy in watching your children develop, being able to put them to bed at night, sharing with them, talking about life . . . great joy indeed."

"But all such good things come to an end," I said, "sooner or later."

"There's a book out entitled *Celebrate the Temporary*." Harold remarked. "I really like that idea. All you've got with your kids is this one moment, right now. You may never have another one. To be living in the future all the time is very foolish. Or to be living in the past. Maybe one of the kids *will* develop personality problems or enter into a marriage that will make him/her miserable. Yet you can't let the future blackmail your joy of the present."

"I'm glad to learn that you aren't going to be all rosy and such in this book," Jeanette commented. "Harold and I know the good times won't last forever. But so much published today gives the wrong impression—that being a Christian is all joy. I have a born-again friend who is going through a very difficult time because her child was scarred from injury. She's not accepting my counsel very well. Why? Because my life is so steady. She has said, 'Oh, well, it's easy for you to say. You haven't faced any of this.' But if I came to her as the mother of a child who has had his face permanently scarred, and I had to have psychiatric counseling, well, she might want to hear from me. But how can I be helpful to other people with problems if I haven't had severe ones myself? A book is the same way. It can't be done as a high and happy one, bursting with joy on every page. There must be sorrow. There must be anguish. These are a part of life. I'll encounter them sooner or later. And I'd want to read a book that shows me how to face such moments—by people who have been through it all."

Next we discussed the sex obsession so prevalent in society.

"Our culture says that we should be sexually stimulated virtually all the time," Harold remarked.

"And if you're not, dump your lover and go to somebody else," I observed.

"Right. It's all so artificial. Permissiveness, the opposite of fidelity, seems to have come into its own these days," Harold said.

"It seems incomprehensible to millions of people," Jeanette observed, "that it is possible, even pleasant, for two persons of the opposite sex, during marriage, to have evenings when they are lying in bed beside one another and do not become sexually aroused. Just to have Harold nearby, to have my head next to his chest, well, that's all I need many nights. The same goes for him. Our relationship is based upon so much more than sexual activity. Neither of us feels the overwhelming need to have intercourse every single night."

She thought of the TV commercials that proliferate these days: "If somebody puts on such and such shaving lotion, and it doesn't cause a woman to become aroused, stimulated, then there is something wrong with her or the lotion or both."

"I remember reading in a national magazine about this actress who said, 'Well, I was married to this guy for ten years, but then I fell in love with somebody else and went off with him.'

"I was angry when I read that comment. Angry because it was supposedly a family magazine, and an *influential* one."

"So casual," I continued. "Like getting a divorce because you've allowed yourself to fall in love with somebody else. Suddenly the marriage ceases to be worth any effort to hold it together. When you fall in love with somebody other than your husband/wife, automatic termination of the marriage should follow. No self-control involved. No dedication to making it work."

Jeanette told me then, "We believe so strongly in our commitment to one another, to the children. Why, certainly, we've said to each other, you can get physically attracted to another person, another body. Okay, that's understandable, that you could have this fleeting moment of attraction. But to be so undisciplined as to let those fleeting impressions get out of control, dwell on them, letting them dominate you, well, that's not something that speaks well of any individual."

She added, "Marriage is not a relationship that requires daily excitement. And you can't *expect* such. Instead you have this fantastic feeling of being *committed* to one person, as he is committed to you. I have the security of total faith in Harold, knowing that he won't run out on me. He will not ditch me for a temporary involvement with someone else. It just makes me so relaxed. I mean, our relationship is so much more relaxed because of that trust we have.

"How great it was for us to get married and have intercourse the first time—for each of us only in marriage to one another. Part of my greatest joy in sex is due to the fact that it's been shared only within our marriage, only with each other. It makes sex between us a lot more beautiful. A lot more. We have no guilt from the past lurking in our minds."

"Even the secular world is, to a degree, coming to realize this," Harold offered. "The superficial approach to sex doesn't work. Just last night, on television, a song was being sung that said it's a tough time for lovers. Everybody's splitting up, and they're saying, 'I've got to be me, without you.' The song very clearly showed how shallow it is to be always thinking of me, me, me. Because that's what it is. I want *my* desires satisfied.

"The secular love songs either deal with just breaking up or promising 'eternal love.' Society's values are contradictory. Permanency is part of man's nature, and when he goes against that nature, he's in deep trouble."

He paused, then: "Nobody is going to be able to partake of everything, as though life is a giant buffet. I am not going, unless Jeanette dies, to ever be able to marry a blond. Or marry a redhead. I maybe will never see the Chinese wall. But our culture says that each human being should be able to grab a piece of everything, feeding our insatiable appetites, take of every great dish from the French chefs, have the most variety sexually. Get. Get. Get. Experience. Experience.

"Yet the Bible says that man's role is to glorify God. We have tasks to do. Some may be boring or unpleasant in other ways, but we simply cannot flit away from responsibility because it no longer *captivates* us. We're not to just taste, taste, taste. Man views himself, or is viewed by other men, as a giant receptacle. We're tied to our TV sets, little blobs on couches. Receiving, receiving, receiving, receiving. We pack in whatever secular manipulation cares to feed us. And they don't realize, they cannot comprehend psychological truth, let alone divine truth. Your sensors begin to deaden in time and you have to keep increasing the dosage, expanding the experimentation, on and on, the frenzy amplifying until it destroys you. Christians must beware of all this."

Ruth Narramore

Clyde Narramore has probably helped more individuals overcome their psychological problems than any other man alive. His Narramore Christian Foundation is a ministry with an outreach that is international. The ten-acre site on which it stands was donated many years ago by a wealthy Christian. There were no strings attached to the transfer of ownership, except one: Clyde could never mortgage the property.

Ruth and Clyde Narramore are two of the nicest, most loyal friends I've ever known. Ruth possesses a youthful personality and vitality that wears out even a mid-thirties guy like me from time to time. Her success as a wife and mother is shown in her family and their life-style.

They work together, these two—write books together, share counseling responsibilities, etc. Over the years they've been very gratified by the success the Lord has enabled them to have as parents of two fine, exceptionally talented children: Melodie, 24, and Kevin, 19.

Why do you think your children turned out as good as they did, which is mighty good indeed?

Well, I know it was the Lord. He gives us directives and ways that we should train our children. If we follow these, we'll be doing the job correctly right from the beginning.

But other Christians have not been as successful. Their children haven't turned out as well. Why is this so?

People will say to us, "Oh, you have all the answers because of Clyde's work; it must be great to be in that kind of situation." I always reply that my children are very normal, just like the children of those who have made that comment. I wouldn't want them not to be normal. They are just like every other child, and they have the same problems, the same joys, the same things to cope with that other children do.

Dedicating the whole family to the Lord is one aspect of parental success. But you can be dedicated to Him and still not have as good a relationship with other members of your family as you should. The spiritual and the psychological both must be handled properly when you are bringing up children.

Have Melodie and Kevin ever manifested the normal aspects of youthful rebellion?

Every child rebels because he doesn't want to do what he is told. I guess our kids had minds of their own. I would expect them to have their own identities, their own outlooks on life, goals to reach, and so on.

When they were little, I used to physically discipline them. But the effect is different with each child. With Kevin, I found that actually spanking him didn't seem to be too effective. In his case, taking away a privilege achieved what I had in mind.

The privileges that were lost included not going to some place that he or Melody (if she were the one involved) had been looking forward to; or not watching some special TV program; that kind of thing.

Actually I'm a bit of a softie, and I've never liked to punish.

How would you answer ultraconservative believers who would be amazed that you ever let them watch TV?

I think we have to realize that television is here to stay, like many other things we have in our culture today. I mean, if we

185

carried things to extreme, we might say that electricity is bad because it turns on the television set.

In life you have to learn controls. I think it is a learning experience for a child to realize that he or she cannot watch just about everything. There are priorities and taboos that must be considered.

We're living in a very wicked age and parents have reason to be concerned.

Were you strict as to the hour at which they had to be back home each evening?

I think that perhaps I was a little more lenient in this respect. I remember when Melodie was in high school and she was first starting to date. This boy came and asked if she had any dating restrictions. So she came and asked me, "Mom, do I have any restrictions?" I said, "Well, I think your restrictions are those you have been learning all your life. You know what's expected of you, and you know how to behave, and you know what is a reasonable time to get home. I'm not putting any other restrictions on you other than those you are aware of already. But if you violate these, I will be very strict about the matter."

It's better, in my opinion, if such restrictions can be taught throughout the formulative years rather than heaped on the young person all at once. This way it's all a basic part of their life.

Who is generally more extroverted, Melodie or Kevin?

That's an interesting question. When Melodie was very young, she was quite shy, and I sort of understood her better than I did Kevin. I think I can understand him now, too, but I didn't early on. I myself have been quite shy. I didn't enjoy it. I wasn't shy because I wanted to be. I was afraid to be otherwise. When I got out of that pattern of behavior, I was very, very happy. Hence, I knew what my daughter was going through. I kept encouraging her. Then when she got into college, she really came out of it, and now she's very confident and feels as though she can conquer the world.

Kevin has always related well with older people—anyone who has a few years on him. I have been concerned that he hasn't done as well with his peers. I was particularly concerned during those earlier years when he should have been mixing more than he did. But he's coming along much better now.

Do you think young people are a special object of Satan's attack?

Satan will attack anywhere he thinks he can get a foothold. I think Satan is especially interested in young people. If he can get hold of a young person, he can potentially influence the world, because young people will become leaders one day.

I think Satan's attack has intensified all over this planet during the last decade or so.

I remember one night that Kevin was watching a program, and I was in another room, working. At some point I came into the living room and saw what he was watching. I said, "Kevin, do you think that that is really going to be helpful to you? Do you think that when you look back on this program it's going to be something that will draw you closer to the Lord or not?" And he replied, honestly, "Probably not." He decided not to continue watching the program.

The point is that, today, young people fill their minds with a lot of intellectual junk food. If Satan can't hit a young person with morally debasing stuff, his second line of attack is that which is so trivial and nonsensical that it causes impeded mental development. An incredibly high percentage of college graduates, for example, are functionally illiterate.

Do mothers exclusively come to you for counseling? Or do the kids themselves occasionally do so?

Both groups do. That's one of the neat things, you know, learning problems from each side of the situation. It also shows that not all kids distrust older people and their advice.

As I look back on the cases I've been involved in, I guess the biggest thread running through them has been that, lots of times, people just have the wrong attitude toward their children. They come to think of them as burden, or as work. And that's sad.

I know that, because Melodie, Kevin and I have had such a great relationship over the years. They have never felt hesitant in coming to me or their father with whatever has been bothering them that they just couldn't seem to work out themselves. Also, you know, this has been true of their friends, too. They would come to me or Clyde and want to talk out their own problems.

At one conference, Melodie brought in this girl and she told me all about how her parents did this-that-and-the-other-thing. They were so strict, even opening her mail, and she was very upset about it all. At first I just sat and listened. That's the first, most important thing you have to do, simply *listen.* You can't judge anything or give advice until you've heard as many details as possible. Even then you've heard only one side of the story. I don't believe you can make a good decision about anything unless you have all the facts. Yet most of us don't have all the facts, though we go on making decisions anyway.

After this girl was through, I said, "Well, I can understand how you feel, and I think, as a person, I would feel upset if somebody read my mail, and did all those other things, too. But I think you need to analyze your parents a bit more. Why are they doing this? I mean, always we have to find the motives. Is it because they don't like you or is it because they're concerned about you, and think that perhaps you need help at this stage in your life?"

Well, after reasoning along these lines, she began to see that maybe what they were doing wasn't right, but it was because they loved her. She began to feel a little better toward her parents. Now the parents needed someone to talk to them, too, and tell them what they were doing wrong.

Parents and children simply don't understand one another much of the time. They don't bother to do so. It's not the child's responsibility, though, to establish such a relationship of understanding. It's the parents' responsibility.

Do you think there is enough emphasis in churches on the needs of single young people?

We have a lack, a big lack. Some churches seem to treat the single as though there's something wrong because they're not married, and that only serves to perpetuate the problems further.

At what age do you think parents should be starting to restrain their control and give more freedom?

It depends on the child and the situation. It's not something that happens all of a sudden. Parents have to be wise enough to detect when the apron strings should be untied.

You know, I don't encourage young people to leave home at a certain age, just because society sort of expects it to happen. I think it depends on why the young person is home. If he's home because there are people who love him and he enjoys being with them, and it's a good place to stay for a bit, why not? Why run around some place else and let your parents wish you were home, and you feeling the same way, if it's not something *any* of you really want? You would be better off at home.

Berdyne Floren/Betty Hanson

NOTE: My original intention was to interview just Berdyne Floren. But Berdyne mentioned her sister Betty several times. Since Betty lived only about ten miles from my own home, we decided that it was a good idea to visit with her also. This chapter alternates between the two women and their interviews.

It was a day much colder than usual for California. The sky was dark, cloudy, and the ocean choppy. But none of the somber people on the small boat were on a pleasure cruise.

The minister had just disposed of the ashes and was turning to the other passengers when the sun broke through for an instant, its rays spotlighting the beautiful colors of a monarch butterfly.

"But what can I say?" Berdyne disclaimed. "I'm just an ordinary person. What advice can I offer?"

After dinner, with Myron going into another room because he wanted the occasion to be entirely his wife's, we sat down in the living room of their home in Southern California.

"Have you ever fallen into the trap of taking your kids for granted?"

"I would never do that!" she declared. "I used to just sit and look at them because I always felt that the day was going to come when they weren't so young anymore. I've always appreciated them. I was never thrilled to death when summer vacation was over, because I hated to see the time come to an end when we could be together more often than when school was in session."

She added, "My sister's experience taught us to *live* every minute you can with them. Betty's son Marty died just a few months ago."

One day after Thanksgiving. Sitting around the table. Having prayed together. Good times. The last Thanksgiving for Marty.

"It happened at the gas station where he worked. He was crushed to death. But Betty's still able to praise God."

* * * * *

"His chest was caved in," Betty was telling me against a Swiss-like backdrop of towering mountains. "He may never have been able to lead a normal life.

"He was dead when we got to Westlake Hospital. My husband and I were shuffled around for quite awhile, and I kept saying to Ken, 'I don't want to stand here. I want to see him.' Then the doctor came and very quickly, but compassionately, told us that Marty was gone."

But the truth doesn't really sink in until you go home and stand before your son's empty room.

"You think you can handle it pretty good until you open that door and look in and go back again and again—and realize that he'll never be there again.

"We just had a river of people coming through to see us in the days that followed. They came to help us, to love us, just to be around, maybe to talk, maybe to cry with us. I never realized how important these post-funeral moments were until I encountered them. In the past I'd shied away from visiting the bereaved because I thought they needed to be alone. But I was wrong. Being alone comes later.

"He was such a sweetheart. Of all the children he seemed the most easygoing. He had always been so agreeable. Maybe he would have changed later but I doubt it. If he were angry about something, he kind of kept it to himself. He might go off to his room for a bit, and then he'd come back and was all cheerful again. So neat."

A fund was created in honor of Marty—money donated to it instead of being spent on flowers. More than $2,500 was accumulated.

"Losing Marty has been quite a sobering experience for us," she admitted. "My other son is at the teen rebellion stage. Marty's death was really an eye-opener. Though he has a place of his own now, he stayed here for three or four nights right after the accident. While he was here, his friends never even missed him nor did they even say anything about Marty. That really hurt him. He's coming to realize that a family can be counted on in virtually any situation. No other relationships are as sturdy, as meaningful."

*   *   *   *   *

Berdyne lives her Christianity. It is not a superficial thing to her, partially why she and sister Betty have been so close over the years. Apart from growing up together, they have worshiped Christ together, and they have cried together.

"Being a Christian was a way of life," Berdyne said. "It's your duty to be as Christlike as possible—to be the right example to the members of your family.

"But for me there wasn't any moment of blinding revelation. I wish sometimes that I could say it was all exciting and ecstatic, but it wasn't. I'm not the sort of person who gets into emotional trips."

Nor are Randy, Christy, Robin, and Holly—the Florens' children. They all profess Christ as Savior and Lord. They display the salvation that is theirs, but not through wild demonstrations of hand-waving, feet-stomping, shouting chaos.

The Christian life of the Florens has been allowed to develop slowly, maturing in the right way. Preparing them for Myron's fight to stay alive back in 1975.

"He just about died," Berdyne recalled. "He had a very, very serious illness. You see, he has this heart valve damage due to rheumatic fever he contracted as a child, but not just once. He got the fever several times; the first was when he was quite young. There were no miracle drugs then, and heart damage resulted.

"He was running a low fever for three months, and that wears on the system. He was taking some medication, yet that didn't seem to help. Finally he got so sick just before Christmas that he went into the hospital. He had an inflamation of the lining of the heart. Only people who have had rheumatic fever come down with that. He was on the critical list for some while before he recovered."

Myron was told by his doctors to take it easy, get eight hours of sleep each day, and so on.

"That's a laugh," she told me. "He works just as hard as he ever did. It *is* frightening to me sometimes the pace he keeps.

"I honestly think the Lord will get Myron to slacken up on the activity before it's too late. We both trust Him with our lives."

* * * * *

Betty has been confronted by people who have insisted that the only reason Marty died was that he or she or both of them had unconfessed sin.

"They probably meant well, but isn't that a terrible suggestion to offer? We have tragedies because we live in a violent world. We build cars that go too fast, and we sell liquor that makes people lose control."

She was alluding to the actual circumstances of the accident, which involved another person. To protect that person she asked that the details be withheld. He is "turning around," as she said.

"Did you feel peace at the time of the memorial service?" I asked.

"Quite a bit. I am really surprised at myself. I have said for years that we never know how we are going to react to any given crisis situation until we are going through it. I always thought I couldn't face the day I had to say good-bye to a close member of my family because of their death.

"It is kind of amazing how God prepares you sometimes," she started to add, then stopped to dry some tears that had formed.

"Don't be embarrassed," I told her. "It's better to express yourself rather than hold it in. People seem to be ashamed of tears in our overly technological world."

"Because my husband and I were going into a new business," she continued, "and since we had never had a good will, we thought it was about time. So the subject of death and funerals and all that was discussed here one evening. Marty spoke up and half-seriously, half-jokingly said he just loved the ocean, loved surfing and swimming, and didn't ever want to be buried. He said, 'I want to be sprinkled on the ocean.' "

* * * * *

"Do you think Betty's faith is stronger because it's been tested," I asked Berdyne.

"It was a shock certainly," she replied. "Her beliefs are almost exactly the same as mine. But as the Bible says, tribulation worketh faith and faith worketh patience. A faith tested in fiery crucible is, I think, a stronger one. That's what Betty's been through. I've been very content in my life and, while I don't take my children for granted, as I said before, Marty's death has taught me to appreciate them even more.

"How suddenly our lives change. The only rational way to go through life with any stability is to put our trust in Him. He has promised never to leave us nor forsake us.

"I think too many people have a faith that is, in effect, put into a box. They know it's there, and the knowledge that it is comforts them. But they never feel the need to take it out of that box until some crisis threatens. I couldn't approach faith in that manner. It has to be a daily, living experience as far as I am concerned.

Berdyne has been concerned about the world in which her children are making their way: "The violence mostly is what upsets me. I read in the newspapers or hear on the radio or see on TV so much about stabbings, mutilations, beatings, rapes, all the rest. I just can't fathom real cruelty, from one person against another. I've never been able to tolerate that. I tried to make sure that my children didn't grow up with any such tendencies. TV shows that were guilty of propagating violence simply weren't encouraged in this family."

Berdyne found the next matter a bit difficult to discuss. It was the essence of a situation deeply personal and tinged with regret.

"Randy was married at nineteen and went away to Texas. It didn't work out and she was back home in four years."

"Were there any children?"

"No. She has since remarried."

"How traumatic was it for you and Myron?"

"Not so bad. We could see that she wasn't happy and it just wasn't working out. I mean, we came to realize that a divorce was inevitable."

"Were you relieved?"

"I don't think I'd put it that way. But Myron and I both realized it was the right thing because she was so unhappy. She called home frequently, but she didn't really complain because she isn't that kind of person. She's kind of stoic, but you could tell that she was hurting. Their life-styles and personalities were completely different. Randy is very, very family-oriented and her husband wasn't. He didn't have the background of traditions that she did. She was far, far away from home, among strangers, and at such a young age. She was faced with a triple assault on the stability of marriage."

"You seem to be a very warm, loving mother. How difficult was it for you to let go?"

"It wasn't terribly hard. I was glad to see they were developing well enough so that they could go out and lead their own lives. This doesn't mean that I am unconcerned, obviously."

We approached the subject of abortion next. Berdyne is not in favor of it, as far as she is concerned, because of several reasons.

"The first is conscience. I just couldn't take that responsibility on myself. I think God is the one to determine whether a child, unborn or otherwise, is to live or die.

"Another is that we never know what we have denied the world by all these abortions. Aren't there supposed to be a million a year? Suppose just one child could have been somebody truly important—there is no way of knowing. The idea that a woman who conceives as a result of being raped shouldn't be forced to bear that child has some appeal. But even here it's certainly not the child's fault that the mother has been violated. How do we know even that child, the child of a rape, might not be a genius that brings our world to some new discovery? I would hate to be faced with the ramifications of that decision. I've told my children, again and again, that there's never anything significant that we do that doesn't affect someone else . . . unless you're the last person alive on earth."

She paused, then added, "We've talked about some heavy matters, but I hasten to add that my life hasn't been heavy, so to speak. Life has been good. I'm happy today. So is Myron. So are our daughters. We are grateful to the Lord for His blessings. Oh, yes, life is good."

"But not perfect?" I asked.

"It never is," she replied. "There have been some things I could wish were changed."

"What are those?"

"Having Myron on the road so much. But I don't worry about this as much as I used to do. Not about him or the youngsters."

"What changed you? Was it any particular thing you did?"

"Oh, I'm not completely changed. I still worry—just not as severely. You see, I was in bed a few months ago, and I suppose I was sleeping. Yet I'm not sure. Perhaps I was dreaming. When I awoke from it, I had this strange feeling of peace which I hadn't had before going to bed that night. It was something really remarkable. I seem to recall someone saying to me, 'Let them go.' When I woke up, I felt just completely at rest about my worries.

"I've been the kind of person who, when members of my family leave the house, I say, 'Drive carefully. Do this; do that.' They're going to drive carefully anyway, but I have had this feeling that if I didn't tell them to be careful, something would happen to them, and it would be my fault. Maybe I've been too much the mother, the wife. What if they get into an accident? What if? You know the syndrome I'm talking about."

"When did you have this 'dream' of yours?"

"Not long before Betty lost her Marty."

*   *   *   *   *

"It's amazing how God works in our lives," Betty was saying toward the end of our time together. "He gives each of us beautiful gifts at just the moment when these are needed, to buoy us up."

. . . the sun broke through for an instant, its rays spotlighting the beautiful colors of a monarch butterfly.

Margaret Taylor

You and Ken have ten children. Are you satisfied with the results of your years of raising them, giving them all the guidance of which you were capable? Or do you have regrets?

We have some regrets, yes. There have been problems we didn't anticipate when the children were small. But we're finding, unfortunately, that these are rather common among other Christian families also. So we're not alone, by any means.

We have had to cope with divorce and alienation. We don't know the cause in the latter instance, and that's what really hurts. Within the last year there has been some communication between this member of the family and another member. But that's all. For a time we didn't know whether our child was dead or alive. The uncertainty is what is hardest to endure.

Any inkling at all as to what happened?

Well, there was an earlier marriage that ended in divorce. Our youngest felt that it would be better to disappear than involve the rest of us in the publicity. I don't want to go into further detail except to say that God seems to be answering our prayers. There is yet some hope for a reconciliation. It's not coming as soon as we've wanted, but it's coming.

Do you have parents coming to you or Ken with their problems?

They don't come to me, and only occasionally to my husband. We don't feel that we have the gift of counseling or the kinds of personalities even that would attract people in this manner. We haven't encouraged any of this.

That's interesting. You say you don't have counseling-type personalities. What sort do you have that would discourage people from seeking you out for this reason?

I think we are very private people. So much so in my case—and perhaps this is a lack of self-confidence—I have never even taught Sunday school. I know that you would suppose I'd be suited very much for this, what with so many children in the home. But it just isn't the case, strangely enough.

We have never been sponsors of a youth group, even when our own children were in their teens. We didn't feel that we had this gift. That would be at least part of the reason. The other part would be due to the number of children in the household. I would be leaving some at home while going off to church or camps with the other children who would be entrusted to me if I got into teaching and such. We didn't have the relatives around who could take over if I wanted to do anything like this, or if Ken and I wanted to go away for a retreat. Furthermore, we didn't have the funds for sitters. So we could find all kinds of excuses to rationalize our lack of confidence. (Laughter) But I do think that if you have the right personality, excuses won't prevent you from teaching or whatever. Instead you would *find* opportunities.

Before "The Living Bible" was published, how was your economic situation?

Let's say it was below average for the suburb in which we lived.

With ten children ultimately, how did you manage? What did you have to do to make ends meet?

We drove very old cars. Except for my husband's clothes, almost everything came from rummage sales or resale shops. I just haunted these places over the years.

We bought day-old groceries whenever possible, and marked down fruits and vegetables in dented cans. We never lacked for food, but it was a simple diet. I was a home economics major in college so I had a little preparation. I was conscious of nutritional values, what constituted a balanced meal, this kind of thing.

We had very, very firm budgets that we had to adhere to in those days. But this wasn't a curse. Husbands and wives often disagree about how to spend disposable income. Ken and I never had that problem, because there was no disposable income. (Laughter) But we were not in debt and we paid cash; we had no credit cards.

You had a budget drawn up and let's say, at the time, you had four or five children. That budget didn't permit any disposable income because no money was left over. Then you had another child, and another. Each time new financial obligations were added. How in the world were you able to adjust an unadjustable budget?

There was an occasional raise in my husband's salary, and it just about grew parallel with the growth of the family. In other words, our circumstances did not improve but we never had real want in any of the necessities.

What did you do for amusement? Recreation?

All of our children are avid readers. We're grateful for that. We never had television, so they turned to books instead. I'll tell you this: I could be a good crusader against TV altogether if I felt I would get a fair hearing. I am embarrassed by what I see from time to time when we turn on the set in a motel room.

With so many children, as close in age as they are, you have enough people to play any game you want, indoors or outdoors. You can play baseball, touch football, whatever. Obviously, with that many youngsters, if you're out in the yard, you're going to have the neighborhood children over, too. So our yard was usually the center of activity, our home entertainment center. We have lived here on this very property for thirty years. We tore down the smaller house some time ago and built this bigger one. It was about the same cost as moving and buying a house already built. Then we had the advantage of tailoring it to our needs.

But, originally, we hadn't been thinking of building. When we went to look at existing houses that had five bedrooms, which is what we thought we needed, I couldn't get my husband out of the car most of the time to give the houses even a fleeting look. He would say, "No yard!" You see, he was used to this full acre with vacant land part of it. We have so much more space than is the case today or even thirteen years ago when we decided to build.

Where did you put everybody in the old house?

Well, initially, the boys slept on the front porch when we closed it off, eliminating the front door and putting new siding on. Before that, everybody, including the girls, slept in two-tiered bunk beds. When Ken's father came to live with us, we had absolutely no room for him, so we added on a new room just for his own use.

What did that do to your budget?

I think we refinanced the mortgage at that point to give us the money. Ken's father lived with us less than two years before he died. When he left us that opened up another bedroom, and eased the pressure, so that the baby didn't have to sleep in a crib until she was hitting the ends.

Did you have so many children because you really wanted them or because you didn't believe in birth control?

It had nothing to do with birth control, actually, although we would have liked not to have believed in it. Let's say that we would like to have trusted the Lord completely for as many children as He wanted to give us. Yet we kind of changed our minds eventually, due to the pressures of life. We decided we just couldn't afford any more offspring.

However, it doesn't mean we weren't using birth control intermittently throughout the years of having our children. What worked for others, though, simply didn't work for us. If there was a five percent chance of pregnancy, then we ended up in the five percent column, time after time.

Then, too, age came to our rescue.

With so many personalities under one roof, do you think, in the final analysis, that this helped in the case of each individual child or tended not to help? Is it better for each child to have so many?

It was a good, close family. Much love was present. Each child was the next child's best friend. This sense of togetherness still abounds, except in the one instance mentioned earlier. They always want to get together, to share, even today.

Our family reunions are really something!

Getting back to TV for a moment, what difference would it have made in the family circle?

The great emphasis on materialism would have been counter-productive, I'm sure, a ripple-like effect. TV tends to draw individuals away into self-contained little environments. It's not a medium that has any favorable impact upon intelligence, morality, whatever. We are as strong today as we are because TV was never allowed to eat away at us.

By the way, in case you get the impression that we simply labeled TV *verboten*, a circumstance the children *had* to live with, I should point out that it was a decision with which they agreed. By and large they are continuing to apply it in their lives away from our home.

Was privacy a rare situation during the growing up years?

All of our *living*, the hours not spent in school or sleeping, were mostly spent in one room, because of the limitations of the house. It was an old-fashioned living room, and that's where they had to practice their music, study, play, roughhouse. The bedrooms were too small, too cold in winter, too hot in summer, for them to siphon off to their own rooms. They literally grew up together.

Did you ever have any of the youngsters come to you and say, "Mom, I just can't stand it. I don't have any privacy."

No. Some of them, after they were grown and were exposed to the problems as delineated in books of psychology and child-rearing, thought it must have been worse, in retrospect, than it really was. And they tried to put some guilt on us, which we refused to be burdened with, because we didn't sense it in any respect at the time.

You said earlier that you and Ken are private people. Why is that? What makes the two of you so private?

It's hard to tell. We've always been that way. Ken, for example, just doesn't make friends easily. He's shy. For years the children tended to be the same way, though most of them are blossoming out very nicely now.

For Ken the work of doing the paraphrase was so time-consuming, so isolating. Over a period of fourteen or fifteen years, he didn't allow himself any diversions. He spent every available minute on it, even during the weekend, because he knew he was doing God's work.

Wasn't that kind of dedication at counterpoint with his responsibilities as a father though?

I don't think so. After all, he was in the house while doing it, and always available if he were needed. The kids are grateful for the contribution their father has made to the cause of Christ. Besides, you can't go back and do anything over again.

Do you see much of your youngsters these days?

They come and go. They feel free to pop in whenever they want. One of my daughters is going to do a painting on this big tray that the kids are making for Ken. Then he can serve me breakfast in bed on Saturdays and Sundays. He serves me breakfast in bed now, but he ends up hunting around for something to use, not having a tray as such. I have to chuckle a bit when I realize, after so many years of marriage, that Ken still has to hunt for utensils, etc. because he doesn't know where such things are. Here he is, a little befuddled, bringing me breakfast and saying, "Why don't we have a decent tray? I can't get it all on this little thing."

With the world we have today, do you ever worry about the future as far as your children are concerned? About what will happen to them?

By nature I am not a worrier. I don't think that means I am free of concern, because I do feel concern. Nor does this mean that I have extra-strong superhuman faith. I just am not worry prone. My husband worries more than I do. You can't change these traits usually. Some people seem to be born with worrying genes.

But it's not worry over how the children will turn out. I think Ken feels, has always felt, that a Christian home was/is the answer. We're a little less sure of that than we were, because of what we have experienced since days when everyone was home together.

Yet deep down we have a certain security, we do feel confident that those who made a Christ-centered decision earlier in life, and were exposed to the teachings of the Bible, will eventually come around and we'll be back with one another again.

But doesn't the Bible say, "Train up a child in the way he should go: and when he is old, he will not depart from it"? Your child apparently has departed. Is this a contradiction?

The Bible does not say, in effect, that he will *never* depart. It says, "When he is old." That leaves room for a period of wandering or, as we would say today, trying other life-styles. But the end result is a return to normalcy.

Joyce Landorf

Life in general, even for Christians, is at best a gamble, to use a secular term. The unknown quantities of everyday experience, such as accident, illness, and so on, seldom give any reason to hope that the gamble can be won. It was different before the fall, but one of the prices to be paid for the transgression of Adam and Eve has been these many, many centuries of suffering and uncertainty which worldly authors have dubbed the human condition.

What difference does accepting Christ as Savior and Lord then make? Obviously our eternal destiny is changed from Hell to Heaven. But *in this life* the presence of the Holy Spirit gives us an anchor. When we feel like giving up, and throwing in the towel, the promise of Scripture is manifested in our lives, namely, that we shall not be tempted above that which we are able to endure. If you had asked Merrill Womach, Joni Eareckson, others at some point in their ordeals whether or not this promise was true, they might have been tempted to reply in denial. But the ultimate result proved to be otherwise. They hung on and triumphed, and have reached inestimable numbers of people as the Lord's instruments of salvation because God's Word was believed and *allowed* to work its miracles.

But no one said that becoming a Christian removes us from pain. A mother has joy but, yes, she has sorrow. She can triumph but she can also be defeated. And disappointed.

Oh, yes, especially disappointed. How many times have mothers the world over cried themselves to sleep because a child let them down, shattered their hopes, perhaps brutally so?

Joyce Landorf has been through a mother's time of desperate waiting—so real and viable that many women reading the truth will readily identify with her.

"From the beginning Laurie was strong-willed," Joyce said, sighing a little. "She was an Rh baby and had to have her blood exchanged twice. She clung so tenaciously to life! Even leaving the hospital didn't mean an end to her difficulties. She got one illness after another when she was a baby, but she seemed determined each time to survive.

"As she was growing up, Dick and I knew we were going to have trouble. There were so many telltale signs—from the delivery room to high school."

It is easy for one to talk about tragedy, hard times, parental frustration if one hasn't been through any of it. You can do so from a kind of ivory tower, passing judgment, offering opinions, and untouched by the anguish. But for those *involved*, opening up this part of life, well, it's a hard decision. Experiences so personal are not easily shared with an outsider.

"The first mother who ever felt as though she had totally failed," Joyce continued, "and who burdened herself with guilt was Eve, when her son Cain killed her other son, Abel. At that point Eve must have said to Adam, 'What did we do wrong? You know, we gave them the same food. We lived in the same tents. They did everything together. They were from the same genes. We taught them. We loved them. We fed them. And now this: Why? Where have I failed, my husband?'

"And I'm sure that God, at some point, must have said to Eve, 'Your son chose to do what he did. He chose not to serve Me and not to worship Me. He chose not to give Me a lamb sacrifice. He gave Me the fruits of his field instead of what I asked.'"

Joyce paused, smiling a little, then: "So, with all this as a prelude, let me say that my daughter Laurie, early into her teens, went into instant rebellion. We could have predicted this. In fact, we could have set our watches by it. We *knew* it was going to happen at some point.

"Oh, she never got into drugs, nothing like that. I think I scared her away from drug experimentation when I came back after singing in an Army mental institution and described what I saw: kids from ages thirteen to nineteen absolutely bombed out of their minds on LSD or some other drug. They were nothings, vegetables, and many would remain that way until the day they died.

"Yet there were continuing, growing upheavals. We had good communication between us for a long time. We were a close family, a loving family early on, but it was rough just the same. She always gave us fits. When Laurie was eighteen, she met and began dating a Christian young man who seemed to us to be a very poor risk. Not only was he wrong for her, but she was wrong for him."

* * * * *

"To put it bluntly," I said, "why did you get involved with him, Laurie?"

We were sitting in my car which was parked in the lot adjacent to United Community Church, Glendale. Her husband Terry was in the backseat with Laurie. I sat in the front seat while interviewing them.

"I thought, when I first saw David, that he was really, really nice," she admitted. "It was a time in my life when I wasn't dating anybody at all. It was fun spending time with him. We just enjoyed being together. And it just progressed more and more into a closer and closer relationship. I honestly thought I was going to marry him for a long, long time."

"Yes, she told me that," Terry said. "I'd come up and ask her out and she'd say, 'David and I are engaged now.' Of course she never had a ring. But she was always engaged, and I'd reply, 'Oh, well, that's nice.' And I'd go away being all discouraged, you know. I'd be sad for a week."

Terry had known Laurie for some time. He felt attracted to her, and it was his prayer that she'd react in the same way about him. But for four long, awful years it seemed as though God had answered his prayers all right . . . with a no.

"David had a lot of weird experiences in Viet Nam," Laurie recalled. "It all made him very much out for himself—to the point *where he wanted his own way, regardless of other people. I would become irritated, and tell him what I thought. His stock reply was, 'Well, you were never in Viet Nam. You don't know what it was like.'*

"*As our relationship progressed, we each became more self-centered, more demanding. As that happened the two of us became meaner and meaner toward each other.*"

*   *   *   *   *

"We began to lose her," Joyce was saying. "She is very beautiful, and yet during that awful period she lost that beauty. The glow just left her. Her sense of humor disappeared. This bright, this warm, this very loving girl, who would weep with me when I was really upset about something, this daughter of mine turned into a quiet, depressed, always sick, always underweight . . . recluse.

"She broke up with him about seven times. It was a terrible time, four years of Hell. We prayed about it, cried together, but, always, she was attracted back to him and would date him again. Much was going on in the relationship that I was very concerned about. I could not accept what I thought Laurie's life-style was becoming.

"So I confronted Laurie with this, and she denied everything. I would talk to her about her relationship with God, and she would say, 'Mom's, it's okay.'

"Then the Lord really convinced me that there was sex going on in her life. So I told her what was on my heart and she replied, 'Absolutely no, Mother. I am fine. Don't you trust me?' Those big, gorgeous blue eyes were looking at me with such sincerity, you know. Yet the Lord was thumping away at the back of my head with, 'Look, I promised I'd give you wisdom and insight, now here it is, lady.' So I was in a real spot. . . ."

*   *   *   *   *

"*I lost at least ten pounds eventually,*" Laurie continued, "*and I had a rash all over my body. It was from nerves and such. I was losing my family, my self-respect, everything—and drifting into a marriage that would be a disaster. I was rebelling against the Lord. It was a pretty bad scene.*"

"I think what Laurie felt for David was really love, though," Terry put in, "at least what she thought was love. Yes, he was

206

lousy to her and, yes, she had many insecurities about herself. But she honestly felt she would be happy with him, that they'd help one another. She wanted to conduct a relationship with someone apart from anyone her parents approved of. It was her choice, her decision, and she thought this would give her self-confidence."

But all the while her self-confidence was being stripped away.

* * * * *

"When I called the college where she was a student," Joyce continued, "and asked for Laurie, her roommate said, 'She's not here.' I asked if she was at class, and her roommate replied, 'Well, yeah.'

"Five minutes later the roommate called me back and confessed to lying. Laurie had gone out to dinner with David the night before and had never returned. 'I'm sure she's staying at his place,' I was told.

"Dick and I hopped into the car, drove to the college, and waited for Laurie to return. By the time she did, having seen our car out front, she was already defiant. She sat on the edge of the bed. When we confronted her with our suspicions, she said that, yes, for two years she had been sexually involved with him. Then she looked at her dad and said, 'Does that make you hate me, Dad?' He gave her the only answer that would have ever clobbered her. I was so proud of him when he said, 'No, Laurie. Nothing you'll ever do will make me hate you. But you know what it does make me want to do?' She said, 'No.' 'It makes me want to go into that bathroom over there and throw up everything I've ever eaten in my whole life.'

"She just burst into tears. She broke up with David right after that, then two days later went back to be with him."

Joyce and I had known each other for a little over a year before this interview took place. I was astonished at her candor. But the situations she was describing were so extreme that only real honesty could give them the impact they had to have in order to help other mothers who might be going through the same thing. You don't earn a distraught woman's respect by beating around the bush. Life isn't beating around the bush when she finds her hopes and dreams shattered in a drama of immoral behavior. That's gut level anguish.

207

"All this time, for four years, I'm praying, 'Lord, are You there? Are You working?' "

Standing in Laurie's bedroom at home. Looking at the dolls from her childhood, the photos showing times of togetherness with her mother, her father, her brother Rick. So much that had been the good, the solid, the *innocent* parts of her life.

No answer.

Lord, are You there?

Nothing.

Lord, is she in trouble? What can I do? Please, please give me some hope. Please—!

Zilch.

"Thanksgiving was a kind of perverse turning point one year," Joyce said. "Laurie came to dinner, and after the turkey and pumpkin, I said, 'Now, Rick wants to talk to you . . . about the cliff that you're going to go over.' So Rick talked to her for twenty minutes, and then Teresa, my daughter-in-law, talked, and my husband—non-verbal Dick—became very eloquent. I said to the Lord, 'Now, what do You want me to say?' And so help me, Roger, the Lord said, 'I want you to be quiet.' And I said to Him, 'Yeah, but I'm her mother and I'm a communicator. I've been speaking to thousands of people. Let me do this.' The Lord said, 'Be still.' He said this three times, and three times I replied, 'No, I won't. I *will* talk to her.'

"So when Dick got through, I wound it all up. I told her exactly why she had to get rid of this man. Why he was ruining her life. I pointed out to her all the broken relationships she had, not only with her family, but her former girlfriends, boyfriends, acquaintances. She needed a healing in her life. When I was all through, she said, 'Okay, Mom. That's enough.' She walked straight out of our lives. The Lord had warned me, yet I disobeyed Him. We all paid for that."

* * * * *

"*The first time I saw Laurie,*" her husband Terry was saying, "*there was this nice, dear, sweet, cute, perky girl. Later she had become unhappy, unsure of herself, just wilting away, skinny, very depressed. The intervals between seeing her made me see the change, the deterioration clearly.*"

"*What was confusing to me is that there'd be times when David would take me out and be real nice,*" she said, "*making me think he was in the process of changing.*"

"It was just enough to string her along, you know," Terry interpolated. "One day he'd treat her real good, the next he'd treat her like dirt."

Laurie wept a little from time to time. At one point I reached over the front seat and tapped her on the shoulder and asked, "Are you okay? Would you prefer not to go on with this?"

She'd wipe the tears away, smile a bit, then continue. "As I think back there's still guilt, I have to admit. I still am dealing with it. Terry says everything is okay, but when you've slipped as much as I have, well, you can't dismiss the guilt easily. I see it going away somewhere in the future, but not yet. I do realize that God loves me, and that the relationship with David is a thing of the past. But, even knowing God has forgiven me, it's a matter of me forgiving myself and, of course, the scars are still there."

In the midst of the worst moments, the nadir of her involvement with David, she came to suspect that not only had she abandoned God but

* * * * *

"The thing I particularly want to leave with readers," Joyce said, "is that, during this nightmare, I did not feel God working. All I saw was that things were getting worse. I saw my daughter dying before my eyes. It was very, very hard for me to believe that God was in control—but He was. He truly was. I asked Laurie and Terry's permission to tell this story. 'Hey, do you want me to share this or not? If you don't, fine. I won't.' They gave me permission. 'Now, Terry,' I reminded him, 'this might be nationwide. Are you sure?' And he said, 'Oh, yes. I want you to do it, Mom. I really do.' We decided that it was right, to tell everything, to show that life for believers is not always one filled with pat answers. Truthfully life is never that way. You're kidding yourself if you make believe that it is. There are times when it is highly possible not to have a single verse of Scripture that makes any sense. Not to have one single friend who can comfort you. Not to have one single moment when you think, 'This really will be all right. This will work out.' I didn't have any moments of hope or peace. I never came to any point during those four years when I was able to say, 'Lord, it is okay. Everything's going to be fine.' No peace. Ever. We were in a state comparable to having the Russian flu every last minute. It was just horrible. And yet—again I must say this—God was working. He was in control. He was doing what He wanted to do. Out of this whole ghastly experience of motherhood, the whole smear,

209

I was finally, finally, finally able to say, my very soul bloody, my mind battered grotesquely, 'You *are* there, Lord. I beg You to forgive me for doubting, for losing control, for calling You, in so many words, a liar, for throwing Romans 8:28 and all the other glorious verses of *promise* down the drain. I am here, Lord, on my knees. Receive me again.' "

* * * * *

"Finally, though," Laurie continued, "I came to realize, in an intimate way, that Christ's death on the cross secured forgiveness of our sins once and for always. Our sins are forgiven. I'm dealing with that now."

She paused, moisture welling up in her eyes again and trickling down the sides of her cheeks.

"I came to the Lord, saying, 'Lord, You know what I've done. I'm deeply, deeply sorry. I ask Your forgiveness.' "

"I just stepped back into the picture at that point," Terry told me. "Our first couple of dates we just went out and had a nice dinner, and then said goodnight. I think it was the third date that we just sat and talked, and talked, and talked. We talked until the sun was coming up, that's how intense the need was to communicate. I had hardly gotten a kiss as yet, and then I finally got a hug.

"It took a lot of hugging, a lot of touching, a lot of just physical contact, you know, getting Laurie to realize that she is a very, very sensuous and a very, very beautiful woman."

"Terry was wonderful. He kept saying, 'Don't worry. Everything will be okay. You are special. You are very, very important, worthwhile to me.' He helped tremendously to heal me. He was loving me in the way I always wanted to be loved, the way I always thought it should be."

* * * * *

Beauty! Was that the seed?

Laurie today is quite beautiful.

She was beautiful *before* the nightmare. She had everything.

Gone! The beauty dissolved so easily; lines formed; bones under taut skin, poking through; circles under eyes, dark, haunted.

"We expect too much of beautiful people," Joyce said. "It may prove to be the worst of handicaps rather than one of the greatest blessings. We expect them to be nice. We expect them to be good. We expect far more from a beautiful person than we ever do from a plain Jane."

210

The interview was almost over. Just a few more minutes. We talked briefly about waiting, about getting old, about—

But nothing, nothing quite so important as the birth, death, rebirth, and inner healing of Laurie Landorf Jacob.

Anne Kennedy

Facing Cancer

I had cancer surgery in 1967; it was very serious. I took cobalt treatments for a month. Cobalt is not the same as chemotherapy. Cobalt is essentially radiation, whereas chemotherapy is a chemical agent. Francis Schaeffer is having the latter. It really affects your body, what he is experiencing. It bloats you. Your hair falls out ... a terrible ordeal. I wouldn't ever take that. I'm sure I wouldn't. The trouble comes when some people have to take both. Eventually your appetite is affected because you're nauseous all the time.

I'm just going the natural therapy route now. After what I've been through, that's the best thing. I think even the controversial Laetrile treatment is better than chemotherapy. I've just made an in-depth study of it and the clinic in Mexico. You see, my dad had cancer also. I took him to a clinic in Jamaica, but he was too far gone when he got there. I think it would have helped him—Laetrile and enzyme therapy together with proper nutrition.

212

The Period of Adjustment

I never had any depression. I never did. It was just a tremendous time, spiritually for me. It really was. I met so many wonderful people in the hospital. I was able to witness to them, share my faith, and tell them why I was able to face having my breast removed without much emotional upheaval.

When James saw me, at home, for the first time, he didn't turn away or anything. He was so understanding and let me know right off the bat that it didn't bother him at all, seeing me as I was.

Cancer—and the Inability to Have Children

We have only one child, and she's adopted. I think my bout with cancer had a lot to do with my inability to give birth. I think it all stemmed from the same problem. In my case it was doctor induced, we're sure. They started giving me hormones in huge amounts, something called Perim, which is now being taken off the market. Some doctor was just using me as a guinea pig.

Telling a Child She's Adopted

From the very beginning our daughter was able to understand the situation. We just told her about the adoption and made her feel special because of it. She said, 'Oh, like Art Linkletter. You know he's adopted, and he mentions this on TV. I'm just like him, right?' She's never asked any questions about her biological mother or father. She's never expressed a desire to find out who they are, or see them at any time.

We didn't tell her all at once but, rather, in stages. She was three years old when we mentioned it the first time. She was told that her mother wasn't able to take care of her; that she wanted her daughter to have a home, a mother and father who could be with her, take care of her real good, and allow her to be raised in a Christian atmosphere.

Even though we're raising her, she does have a somewhat different personality than James or myself. She's "up" a lot more consistently than we are. She is always cheerful, able to just tell you she loves you no matter how or what the situation is, or how she feels that particular moment.

213

Keeping a Neat House

I couldn't live in a sloppy house. I think everything should be kept so that you're not ashamed if a visitor should pop in suddenly. Orderliness is important. Our daughter is like that, too. When I was her age, I don't think I was—that trait came later. She straightens her room up every morning before she leaves for school. And she's orderly in other ways, too.

The Family Pet

My daddy was a veterinarian. We always had a houseful of dogs and cats. I loved them all. We don't have any today because we're gone periodically, and it would be a problem taking care of them. In fact, I just couldn't stand to leave them without their getting the proper care.

When our little dog died, well, it was so hard for me. I still miss her. Pets became part of the family circle. I was dating at the time, and my boyfriends were all jealous of that dog. I seemed to love that dog more than them. Anyway, it was hard to lose that little thing. I guess that's another reason I haven't gotten a dog again, because I'd hate to go through losing another.

Why Florida for the Church?

The Lord just put us here. When Jim was graduated from seminary, he applied for the mission field. He'd been hearing all those sermons about missions and he felt that he had to apply. How could he stand in the church and exhort people to go to the mission field when he hadn't made himself available?

Africa was what he seemed to have in mind. I really didn't want to go. It was just a dumb reason: I thought I'd never be able to use all my pretty wedding gifts, my china and all the rest. I really had to pray about it. I just prayed that the Lord would make me want to go—and He did. He just changed my whole thinking on it. Then we were turned down because James was having asthma real bad!

But this condition corrected itself. Finally, after months of waiting, we were told about a little home missions committee in

Florida who was thinking about starting a church. Maybe we'd like to go down there and be interviewed. That became the first church we ever had.

Her Daughter's Career Plans

She plans to be a nurse. That's what she's had in mind for many years. When she was three or four years old, I gave her a stethoscope and a nurse's hat. She really liked to play with them.

She is eager to help people. She wants to ease their pain and, wherever possible, speed them along the road to recovery. Seeing your child turn out this way has to be one of life's greatest joys.

Nancy Schumacher

Nancy and Paul Schumacher were on the road. Paul is one of the finest gospel singers in the country. Their stops in California were highly successful. We have been friends for a long, long time. We understand one another, and Nancy and Paul are almost surrogate brother and sister to me. One afternoon we walked through Busch Bird Gardens.

Nancy: "I'm just an ordinary, common, everyday mother who has struggled with the normal problems a mother faces," Nancy is saying as my mind recalls.

Roger: "You're more of an authority than someone who has raised no children," I offer.

We walk a bit farther, enjoying the colorful birds, the beautiful vegetation.

Roger: "Have you and Paul often differed on the approach that should apply in raising Marla and Greg?" I ask.

Nancy: "When you have two individuals with different personalities spending life together, you're not going to agree on some things. That's to be expected. There have been times when I felt something should be handled one way and Paul has thought it should be another way."

Roger: "Can you give an example?"

Nancy: "Honey, can you help me?" she asks her husband.

Paul: "Nope," he says, not out of indifference but out of a marriage-long conviction that an interview with Paul is just that or one with Nancy is just that. Each stands or falls by himself/herself.

Laughter.

Even so Paul interjects this comment: "Perhaps you tend to be a little more lenient than I am. I think, occasionally, that things should be handled more sternly."

Nancy: "That's true. I mete out a lesser degree of punishment than my husband does."

Roger: "All right." I sidestep a multi-colored bird that has skittered right in front of me. "Say that Marla has done something wrong. What would your punishment be and what would Paul's be?"

Nancy: "I probably would take her TV away from her. Paul might ground her for a week. She hates that worse than anything—to be totally grounded."

Another pause as we savor the surroundings.

Roger: "Was it easy, Nancy, becoming a mature adult yourself? Or did you have it rough enough to give you some insight into the problems young people face?"

Sing a lonely song for me. I have no one. I need help from Above. Sing a lonely song for me. I hurt, hurt, hurt. . . .

The record sticks. The word is repeated over, over, over—hurt, hurt, hurt. . . .

Roger: "Was it easy, Nancy?"

Nancy: "I don't think anything in life is easy. I don't care what your background may be. When trials and tribulations come, they hurt, really hurt, no matter what. I have envied people who have had a solid heritage, parents who really displayed their love and did anything for you. I've thought what a secure background, what a blessing. But does the lack of that *have* to affect my life? How do I handle my life from that point on? It may affect my emotions in given situations, but does it have to affect the ultimate choices and outcome of my life? I had to decide, for my own survival, that the answer was no."

Roger: "But you had to make that conscious decision. You had to stop and say, 'No more. That's it. Things have got to change—or I'm dead.' "

Nancy: "Right. Absolutely right. There is little in life which we cannot break from if we have the Lord's help. But it does require effort, often supreme effort. You would be lying to yourself if you supposed that twenty years of a certain pattern can be abandoned in twenty-four hours. So many people say, 'I just can't help myself. When I'm with a woman, I gotta take her to bed because that's the way I am.' To me that's simply saying, 'I'm a robot and I have no free will, and I have no ability to choose, no mind of my own.' "

Roger: "Rather like a form of satanic delusion or possession."

Nancy: "Yes, a bit. What is possession if it's not the obviating of our own will and the substituting of control by someone else!"

Roger: "Do you find yourself, today, as a result of what you once endured, clinging to your husband, afraid of losing him?"

Nancy: "In the beginning, when we were newly married, I would say that I was a clinging wife. But I now have the years of security behind me. It never enters my mind that I will lose him unless the Lord calls him home. But reaching that point was—."

Roger: "—like going cold turkey from a drug habit."

Nancy: "Right. It's a growing thing, this distance from the past."

We walk on. It's getting a little colder. We shiver a bit. Soon we will return to the car and continue the interview there.

Roger: "In a sense, Nancy, knowing the mercurial aspects of life, of being a parent, of so many lives combining together, could we say that it's virtually a miracle when everything turns out okay?"

Nancy: "I would only say that the Lord has wrought a great and wonderful thing. I don't think there's any parent today who would say, 'I have done a great job of raising my children.' When you consider that each child is an individual with his own genes and chromosomes and problems, and that anything could happen as a result, yes, it's a miracle when most of what you pray about turns out even remotely true."

Roger: "The pressures. Young people need heroes. And whom do they have today?"

Nancy: "John Travolta—and who does he portray in each film thus far, a young man who sleeps around, who has no regard for

Biblical morality? Yet his impact is greater than anyone since The Beatles. The heroes young people have are the ones that lead the worst, most sinful lives. I wonder to myself, 'Why are they heroes?' Because they have gone out and done all of these forbidden things, and the allure is irresistible. This is true even with born-again celebrities who have given up the filth. Christians flock to them from a kind of perverse fascination with their past."

Roger: "What are the three most serious mistakes one can make as a mother, Nancy?"

Nancy: "Motherhood is difficult. More difficult than being a wife. You're molding character in another person. That's a big responsibility. The least hypocrisy witnessed can reverberate with devastating effect. I think one of the most serious mistakes for me, for any mother, is not treating your children objectively. You are so emotionally involved with them that you cannot be objective. When they do something bad, you react to that emotionally rather than coolly and objectively as you would to someone else's child.

"Because a mother cares so very much for her child and everything that happens to that child, there is a tendency to be possessive. To be conscious of this is good. You can then try to back off and let the Lord work in your child's life to deal with those difficult things that you want to protect him from."

We are in the car now. Driving toward Hollywood. Little smog in the air—not enough to hurt your eyes. We haven't spoken for a bit. Admiring the scenery.

I am intent. Over the weeks of writing this book I have heard of families with retarded children, families with a loved one killed tragically in a plane crash, these and more, agony in a continuous stream, unbroken.

Roger: "Is being a mother worth the pain? Is the joy all that surpassing?"

"In motherhood," Nancy says bluntly, "the pain perhaps seems more frequent than the joy. As I look back comparing recent years with the earlier ones, I do feel that there was more joy when they were small and dependent. Their problems were easy to solve. As they grow older everything becomes more complex.

"But I don't necessarily agree with this. For there are so many mothers who haven't faced tragedy until they see their children become loathsome adults who may murder or rob or rape or whatever.

"I miss so many moments from the early years. Their joys were so innocent. Their joys were my joys. Our daughter loved flowers. Just seeing a flower and stopping to smell it was a real joy to her and so, therefore, it was my joy. Now, as my children are older, and my son is a married man, we don't stop to smell the flowers as we did when they were younger. That's especially a contrast with Marla. She was the flower smeller. She saw every little bug in every little flower. Every little, bitty, bitty bloom was a source of real happiness. Now we don't notice the blooms. You could almost sing, 'Where have all the flowers gone?' It's sad."

Sad, yes. But we go on. Mothers. Fathers. Daughters. Sons. We go on because of the past. Or we go on in spite of the past. New families begin. The cycle repeats. While the grandmother is dying, in a hospital or a home for the elderly, a grandson is out in a field, studying a butterfly. He is called in, told that she has died, and he cries. He goes to the funeral, and there is mourning, but soon that field and that butterfly beckon. Maybe, just maybe his sister will stop to smell a flower.

"If we're fortunate enough," Nancy says, "we learn and we pass what we have learned on to our children. If we have improved their future from what we have experienced in the past, if we can teach them the importance of trusting the Lord totally, that's the greatest legacy of all."

I'd like to paraphrase David of ancient times who said it this way:

Lord, help me to realize how brief my time on earth will be. Help me to know that I am here but for a moment. We glide along the tides of time as swiftly as a racing river, and vanish as quickly as a dream. We are like grass that is green in the morning, but mowed down and withered before the evening shadows fall. Seventy years are given us! And some may even live to eighty. But even the best of these years are often emptiness and pain. Soon they disappear and we are gone. Teach us to number our days and recognize how few they are. Help us to spend them as we should.

Epilogue

It is dirty in Alexandria, Egypt. Alexander the Great would be heartsick with the place. Come to think of it, dirty is really too polite a word. Filthy comes closer even though that seems a bit mild somehow.

As Jerry Falwell, John Montgomery, and I walked the crowded streets, we were astonished at the depth of the poverty. Not Watts or Harlem or any of the other ghettoes in the United States come close in comparison; they are more like places of the affluent class compared to what we saw.

Anwar Sadat recognizes the terrible burdens upon his people—a key reason for his peace initiative. He wants desperately to raise their living standards, to give them a measure of prosperity which they have not known for centuries.

But there is another comparison that could be made—and, with this one, Americans do not come out on top. I saw many, many mothers in Alexandria who were tending to their children: feeding them, laughing with them, washing their faces, being with them in the time-honored way of mothers. The striking thing was that since they had known poverty all their lives they had adjusted to it, and they were somehow happy within its limitations.

"If this is all we'll ever have, we might as well get used to it," was what they seemed to be saying without words. The children would come up to us and tug at our sleeves. Sometimes they asked for money but, incredibly, at other times they were apparently content *just to smile at us!*

Isn't that mind-blowing, to use the modern expression. They were covered with dirt smudges, their clothes were ragged, few had any shoes on their feet, and yet a mere smile, a shake of the hand, would make them ecstatic with joy.

I had a camera with me so I became something of a center of attention. The children, very young as well as teenagers, competed among themselves for the attention of my lens. They danced and jumped and made funny faces—eager to be captured on film and to be viewed by unknown people in that far-off land of America.

A taxi driver took me around to various spots in the country. The countryside was alternately bleak and beautiful, with far more vegetation than I had imagined would be the case.

"Would you like to see my home?" he asked, his face beaming. "And meet my wife and children?"

I said that I would be happy to do so. The man was genuinely pleased with this and took me somewhat off the main thoroughfare to his home, hastily adding as we went, "No charge, sir. No charge. It is my pleasure."

The road, what there was of it, was dusty and riddled with small holes. On either side stretched rolling expanses of green—I wasn't sure what was being raised there—that the man gestured to with a sweep of his hand, indicating that this was his farm.

We stopped in front of what could best be termed a mud hut. It was larger than others I had seen in Egypt, and it seemed a little more elaborate, but a mud hut nevertheless. As we got out of his car, he called to some figures way out in the field to our left. They came a-running.

The woman was missing a couple of her front teeth, and several others were either decaying or bent, but she took my hand and introduced me to her children, delighted that I was willing to meet them.

I took some pictures, and the man invited me into their home for some food. I declined politely, and for dietary reasons. While in Egypt, it is a good idea *not* to drink the water, and not to eat any food except in very good restaurants.

222

He took me back to rejoin the others, and soon afterwards we returned to Cairo. A long meeting went on very late into the night and did not, in fact, end until 4 a.m. We were scheduled to arise at 6:15 a.m. that same morning. After some thought I decided that going to bed, falling alseep, and then awakening after so little sleep would be worse on my system than simply staying up.

I read my Bible for a few minutes and then went outside. The sunrise was beautiful indeed, casting a golden hue over the pyramids which were only a mile or so away.

I started walking and after a short while I approached the pyramids. I sat there, on one of the giant blocks, and prayed. One of the camel drivers who seem to be there at any hour watched me, respectfully, without interruption. When I was finished, and started to get to my feet, he came over to me. After quite a bit of earnest pleading on his part, I decided to ride the camel back.

It walked slowly, as though it had all the history of its nation on its back, weighing it down. Every so often it would turn its head as a car zoomed on by, but continued on, a little weary, green slime coming out of the sides of its mouth.

I saw children again. This time they were with their mothers, occasionally with their fathers as well, walking, packs of whatever on their backs. Their bare feet stirred up dust that smelled much like the inside of the pyramid into which I had partially climbed, partially crawled on my hands and knees—the odor of death and decay, the dust the color of cremated bodies. I would turn my head and look back, and they would virtually disappear into the stuff.

I asked the "driver" why there were so many out on the roads at such an early hour, and he replied, in surprisingly coherent English, "Oh, that, sir, is their way. They go from place to place. You see, sir, they have no home."

I wondered to myself about this kind little man with his dirty body and his ragged clothes and his camel, with which he probably had a most affectionate relationship. Was he like the others about whom he had just commented, no home, merely wandering from place to place, alone, a statistic on the governmental poverty chart. Undoubtedly, at least I imagined so, the man would die before the camel did. The camel would stand there, nudging him, its cute/ugly face uncomprehending. Somebody else would take it on, and maybe it would outlive that man, too. But, eventually, after decades of sameness, the hunger that arises from eating only infrequently, it, too, would bend its knees, as it did to receive a rider, grunting, and it would lie down and never get up again.

But long after I was in Israel, the final leg of the journey, long after I was safely enveloped in a modern, plus five-star hotel overlooking the Old City where Christ spent His last days before being crucified, my mind went back to those children in Alexandria. I thought of that kind taxi driver and his family and those wandering, homeless mothers and their clinging children.

I cried because I had no shoes
Until I saw the man who had no feet.

In Alexandria and Cairo and elsewhere in Egypt, the survival—not the destruction—of the home is of paramount consideration to every mother, no matter how humble her circumstances. For her children are all she has; her husband, too. They are the center of her world. She makes do the best she can, and when a little extra grain is made available, somehow, she accepts it with transcendent gratitude.

Though the poverty is there, though often all she can give her babies is the milk from her breasts, she is happy. Because they are happy. To her tomorrow will be another day just the same as today. But she and they will survive until the day after that, and maybe just maybe that will be the end, malnutrition reaping its terrible toll.

You get the feeling that so long as they can die together, so long as the mother can have her little ones around her, their bodies pressed to hers, so long as she does not have to worry about her end coming first, then she will be singing to them, her voice a melody of comfort until she can love them no more.